Grades 2-6
Seasonal
and Holiday

Springboards & Starters

Written by
Linda Milliken

Illustrated by
Barb Lorseyedi

Cover Design
Wendy Loreen

Cover Illustration
Priscilla Burris

ISBN 1-56472-011-X

Seasonal & Holiday Springboards and Starters © 1993

Edupress • PO Box 883 • Dana Point CA 92629

Table of Contents

SEASONAL STIMULATION
*Ideas to integrate into each season—
in a variety of skill areas and formats.*

Table of Contents

HOLIDAYS ... IN GENERAL

Ideas that adapt to any—and all—holidays.
Discuss, explore, create ... all in the name of holidays.

Table of Contents

HOLIDAY MENU

Learning-rich, activities and projects for specific holidays.
Link with literature ... Work Cooperatively!

Table of Contents

TEACHER HELPERS

Useful tools for quick lessons, classroom environments and motivating students.

Seatwork Jumpstarts — reproducible pages

Bulletin Board Boosts

Inventive Incentive

Index

Working on a theme? Need an idea for a holiday that isn't on its menu page? Look here for complete listings.

PANTOMIME TIME

Sometimes it's easier to act out thoughts instead of speaking. Play a pantomime game to test the theory.

Ask students to act out seasonal activities—no words spoken. Then ask classmates to try to identify the action.

You may want to provide a, list for younger students to choose from. Discussion of seasonal activities prior to pantomime would be helpful, too.

Here's a list of seasonal actions to choose from and add to.

▼ raking leaves
▼ collecting seashells
▼ shoveling snow
▼ playing football
▼ skiing
▼ building a snowman
▼ pitching a tent
▼ husking corn
▼ shelling peas
▼ swimming
▼ bear hibernating
▼ planting a garden
▼ getting on a schoolbus
▼ walking in the rain
▼ putting up an umbrella
▼ putting on mittens
▼ putting on boots
▼ caught in a hailstorm
▼ squirrel gathering nuts
▼ bird building a nest
▼ bird taking a bath
▼ a flower growing

▼ catching butterflies in a net
▼ diving in a lake
▼ boarding a plane
▼ hiking
▼ watching the world series— or superbowl
▼ sunbathing
▼ snail eating a dewy leaf

Quick Pick Talk Topics

Use these prompts for spontaneous, short talks by individual students.
The fun format will put them more at ease.

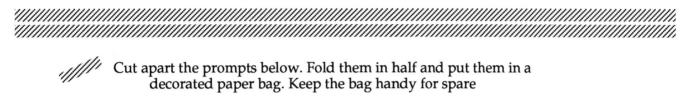

Cut apart the prompts below. Fold them in half and put them in a decorated paper bag. Keep the bag handy for spare classroom moments.

Student reaches in and pulls out a seasonal talk topic for a quick, impromptu "speech" of a just a sentence or more depending on student age and ability.

The season I like best.

Things to do with snow.

Things I like to do on a rainy day.

A good spring cleaning project …

If I planted a garden I would grow …

If I could open a store it would be …

I would like to go on vacation to …

My favorite ice cream in summer is …

I like going back to school because …

When I think of fall I think of …

Who Are They?

Real or imaginary? Who are these people?
Find out ... then talk about your findings.

More to do:
• Assume their "identity" and share a conversation with classmates.
• Plan a day to come dressed as one of these characters.
• Write and present a skit that includes these seasonal "people" as players.

Fall

Mr. Sandman

Jack O'Lantern

Mother Goose

Mariah

Winter

Jack Frost

Father Time

Cupid

Mankind

Spring

Mother Nature

Mr. Clean

Queen of Hearts

Man in the Moon

Summer

Uncle Sam

King Neptune

Hurricane

Andrew

✸ REASONS FOR SEASONS ✸

> *Use these activities to make your students aware that seasonal changes are very clear in some parts of the country but hardly noticeable in other parts.*

✸ Engage your students in a discussion about what happens to certain jobs and occupations when the seasons change. Some jobs <u>change</u> with the seasons; other jobs do not exist at all when seasons change.
   What happens to the ice cream man in the winter?
   What does the ski instructor do in the summer?

✸ Make a list of jobs that only exist in certain parts of the country.

✸ Have students bring in samples of different fabrics and create a "Seasonal Clothing Collage." Label each fabric under the season: FALL: corduroy, wool, knits; SUMMER: light cottons, etc. Have students design the collage in groups to give a balance of color and design.

✸ Arrange an indoor seasonal picnic and serve foods to go with the season: winter (soup and crackers, hot chocolate with marshmallows), fall (turkey and cranberry sauce sandwiches with apple juice), etc.

✸ Have students bring in records or tapes with traditional songs that are about the weather. Assistance from parents may be needed in tracking down songs such as: *Autumn Leaves, Winter Wonderland, Moonlight in Vermont, See You in September*, etc. and other oldies…

✸ Write 'acrostic' poems or descriptions of the seasons. Write one letter per line vertically to spell the season and students use the first letter to begin each line.

✸ As a cooperative class project, have children bring in seasonal fruits and create a salad.

SCIENCE
Through the Seasons

Conduct some seasonally-related scientific studies.

WINTER

- Find out what happens to a snowflake after it falls to the ground.

- Draw a diagram of an iceberg—above and below the water's surface.

- Find out which animals hibernate. Make a chart.

- Follow the path of migrating birds or whales.

- Diagram a constellation in the winter sky.

- Find out the average temperature in the North Pole.

- Make a pair of snowshoes and attempt to walk.

- Find out about penguin life in a rookery.

- Experiment with freezing temperatures. Dip a variety of things in water and place in the freezer. Remove and compare results.

SPRING

- Find out what causes thunder.

- Learn to identify cloud formations.

- Try to build a bird's nest.

- Build a birdbath or bird feeder. Quietly observe.

- Examine insects through magnifying glasses.

- Learn to use a barometer.

- Keep track of the number of daylight hours.

- What is humidity?

- Find out about the ecosystem of a pond.

- Make a map of the water source for your community.

SCIENCE
Through the Seasons

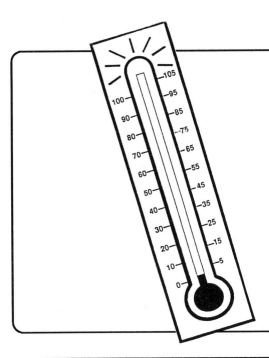

SUMMER

- Draw a diagram of the greenhouse effect.
- Find out about the effects of sun on the skin. Conduct sunblock comparison experiments.
- Experiment with color and heat absorption.
- Learn to read an outdoor thermometer.
- Find out how shells are formed.
- Make a diagram of life at different sea levels.
- Make a sundial and record your observations.
- Conduct melting experiments.
- Examine insulation and explore its effectiveness.

FALL

- Find out why leaves change colors.
- Grow mold.
- Conduct a mushroom investigation.
- Make a leaf compost pile.
- Find out how science has helped farmers.
- Learn about poisonous pesticides.
- Diagram the steps in the process of photosynthesis.
- Find out how corn grows. Husk an ear and examine the parts.
- Conduct leaf comparisons. Make a chart of the different kinds.
- Conduct a pumpkin experiment. Carve one; Leave one intact. Compare the decomposing rates.

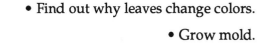

MATH
Through the Seasons

Conduct some seasonally-related math studies.

WINTER

- Study octagons. Make cut-paper snowflakes.

- Learn how to use a calculator.

- Make shopping lists from advertisements. Calculate expenses.

- Build geometric shapes using toothpicks and marshmallows. Save a few for a cup of hot chocolate.

- Cut cookie dough into equal parts. Bake.

- Count the spirals in a pinecone.

- Use baking cups for sorting and counting.

- Plan an indoor game fest. Learn to play checkers.

- Set up a measurement center. Compare liquid and dry measurements.

SPRING

- Take a shape walk.

- Time the travel of a snail.

- Learn to count to ten in another language.

- Estimate and count the petals in a daisy. Compare results.

- Write insect word problems, based on eight legs per insect.

- Examine flowers. Record the variety of petal shapes.

- Time how long it takes an egg to boil.

- Measure the length of flower stems.

- Draw individual hopscotch squares on the playground with exact measurements

MATH
Through the Seasons

Conduct some seasonally-related math studies.

SUMMER

- Learn to read number coordinates.
- Take your body temperature, before and after drinking a glass of cool juice. Calculate the differences, if any.
- Study the shape of a cone. Make and measure a variety of cones. Prepare a snowcone.
- Examine the shape of sails. Paint a sailboat picture to reflect the shapes.
- Calculate the differences between Calsius and Fahrenheit readings on a thermometer.
- Conduct probability tests with a coin. Chart the head and tail tosses.
- Make a yarn sun. Measure the length of the rays before cutting.

FALL

- Estimate the number of leaves in a pile. Count..
- Learn to set a clock.
- Cut an apple pie into fractional pieces. Enjoy.
- Measure the circumference of a pumpkin.
- Measure the length of a variety of squash.
- Use pumpkin seeds to understand place value.
- Measure ingredients for a harvest soup.
- Conduct a leaf size comparison.
- Measure your shadow at different times of the day.
- Estimate the kernels in an ear of corn. Count rows and multiply.

SEASONAL SENTENCES

Read the sentence spark aloud. Encourage attentive listening by reading the sentence only two times. Give students a couple minutes to write a sentence in response. Share your seasonal sentences by inviting a student to write one on the chalkboard. Punctuate, capitalize and check spelling together.

Write a sentence ...

... with three fall colors in it

... with two words that describe a pumpkin

... that describes how you feel on the first day of school

... that a quarterback would say to his teammates

... that describes a school bus

... telling what a snowman might say

... describing the feel of a snowflake on your tongue

... convincing Father Time not to ring in a new year

... with three rainy day words in it

... with two months named in it

... about a way to warm up on a cold winter day

... that tells something about birds

... with a busy insect in it

... describing an unusual flower

... with the word "hibernate" in it

... telling what a bee said to a flower

... containing the words "spring fever"

... about a walk in the rain

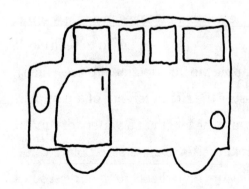

The school bus looked like a big, yellow banana.

Just for fun ...

Choose one of the sentences to illustrate. Everyone can illustrate the same one and compare the results or choose different ones and write the sentence with a caption underneath.

Notes for all Seasons

Reproduce a page for each student. Have them draw a classmate's name out of a bag. Each season, write a special note or paragraph to this same classmate.

Friendly Fall Note

Warm Winter Wishes

Lively Spring Message

Sunny Summer Thoughts

Titles and Topics

Titles

Crazy, Mixed-up Classroom

Dinosaur Goes to School

Field Trip Fantasy

The Talking Turkey

Topics

Why do leaves change color?

What jobs do farmers have in the Fall?

Favorite Fall sports.

Setting goals for the school year.

Titles

My Pet Penguin

The Clumsy Polar Bear

Hibernation Hotel

Wacky Winter Adventure

Topics

What is *hibernation*?

How do animals and people prepare for winter weather conditions?

Life in an Eskimo igloo.

When is it winter in other parts of the world?

Titles and Topics

Titles

The Ickiest Insect in the World

Spring Cleaning Calamity

The Bird That Wouldn't Fly

The Day It Rained Chocolate

Topics

Insects: variety and characteristics

How to plant a garden

Cloud formations

How a bird builds a nest

Spring

Summer

Titles

Lost at Sea

The Sad, Sad Sun

My Dream Vacation

The Lazy Whale

Topics

Water sports

The effects of heat

Ocean life

Vacations: varieties and destinations

Ways With Words

Here are some ideas to help build vocabulary and develop word usage throughout the year.

Word Banners

Make a list of nouns associated with each season.

Then create a list of verbs.

Write them on butcher paper banners to hang on the wall.

Decorate the banners with fancy seasonal borders.

Set aside some space on the chalkboard under the heading

Rhyme Time

Write a new word each Monday. Ask students to write rhyming words as they think of them throughout the week. On Friday, write poems using the rhyming words.

Alliteration

Brainstorm a list of alliterative seasonal adjectives. Here are some examples:

Winter	Spring	Summer	Fall
wacky weird	slimy scrumptious	slippery splendid	funny freaky
wild wonderful	super surprising	suspenseful silly	frightening frantic

Acrostics

Sunny
Unbelievable
Marvelous
Mercury goes up
Eventful
Round trip tickets

r
a
i
n

icicle

Shape-Up

Work in pairs to create shapes to go with seasonal words.

Write the word inside the shape and suspend them from the ceiling with colorful yarn.

Write About Something ...

Life in an Igloo

The Great Popsicle-eating Contest

Caught in a Snowstorm

My Favorite Ice Cream

"These things leave me cold ..."

"They game me the cold shoulder when..."

The dangers of ice and snow ...

Encounter with the Abominable Snowman

Cold Weather Activities

The Runaway Snowman

The truth behind ...

- goosebumps
- chattering teeth
- shivering

A Desert Adventure

Campfire Storytime

What's Hot! What's Not!

Tale of a Fire-Breathing Dragon

Hot Weather Activities

The Day the Sun Wouldn't Shine

Sad Sam the Sunbeam

"He's full of hot Air ..."

"I was sitting in the hot seat when ..."

A descriptive paragraph about

- hot dogs
- hot chocolate
- hot spiced cider
- red hots

Link literature with the seasons. Here are some suggested titles and springboards for related activities.

Seasonal Literature Links

Fall

The Gitter, the Googer and the Ghost by Cherie R. Wyman (gr. 3-5)
Two boys investigate the truth behind a ghost story in an abandoned house.
Write a *cooperative* ghost story. Ask a class member to design a cover and bind it.

Eat Your Peas, Louise! by Pegeen Snow (gr. 2-4)
Fewer than 100 words in a story about a little girl who doesn't want to eat her peas.
Write short stories describing a food that you don't like to eat.

Toasted Bagels by Joyce Audy Zarins (gr. 2-3)
Mouse invites everyone to share his toasted bagels.
Prepare and share a snack of bagels.

Winter

It's Snowing! It's Snowing! by Jack Prelutsky (all grades)
Story poems on the experiences and joys of winter.
Make a list of winter-related rhyming words and write original poems.

Winter Magic by Eveline Hasler (gr. 2-4)
A boy discovers winter's beauty through hearing a story of the winter kingdom.
Paint a picture of an imaginary winter kingdom.

Cutlass in the Snow by Elizabeth Shub (gr. 2-6)
True story about an adventure share by a boy and his grandfather involving pirate tales.
Find out about life aboard a sailing ship in the 1800s.

Seasonal Literature Links

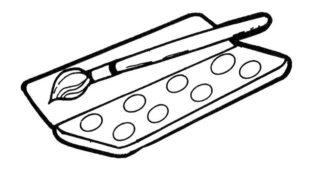

Spring

Busy Buzzing Bumblebees and Other Tongue Twisters by Alvin Schwartz (gr. 2-5)
A book of tongue twisters.
Write alliterative tongue twisters with other spring insects as the subjects.

Egg-Drop Day by Harriet Ziefert (gr. 2-4)
A class finds out there's more than one way to drop an egg out a window and not break it.
Challenge students to devise a way to drop an egg and keep it from breaking. Dye the surviving eggs for spring baskets.

All Wet! All Wet! by James Skofield (gr. 2-3)
A small boy takes a wet walk in the woods on a rainy day.
Color a scene then paint blue watercolor over it to create a rainy day crayon resist.

Summer

Time of Wonder by Robert McCloskey (gr. 2-4)
A story of summer on the Maine coast and the hurricane that hits it.
Find out about the causes of hurricanes and other weather phenomenon.

The Summer Snowman by Gene Zion (gr. 2-3)
Henry keeps a snowman in the freezer and brings him out on the Fourth of July.
Conduct ice experiments in the summer sun. Chart melting time.

The Wreck of the Zephyr by Chris Van Allsburg (gr. 3-5)
The narrator meets an old sailor who tells him an improbable tale.
Write a tale of the sea. Paint a picture to illustrate it.

Seasonal Solutions

Use words, pictures or roleplaying to show some possible solutions for these seasonal problems.
Conduct group discussions to compare and evaluate the proposed solutions.

FALL

- You've raked a huge pile of leaves. What should you do with them?

- Your best friend didn't make the football team and you did. What will you say?

- You don't have a costume for Halloween. What can you do?

- The group want to go in a dark area to "trick-or-treat". What will you do?

- Your aunt serves you a dish that you don't like for Thanksgiving. What will you do?

- You missed the school bus and your parents are at work. What solution can you think of?

WINTER

- You are playing in the snow and your fingers grow numb. What do you do?

- You don't have any money to buy Christmas or Hanukkah presents. What can you do?

- You're sick with a winter cold but an important event is coming up. What will you do?

- You lost your new winter jacket. What will you tell your parents?

- You don't have any store-bought paper to wrap presents. What can you use do?

- You want to send a card to someone special you admire but you're afraid they will laugh. What will you do?

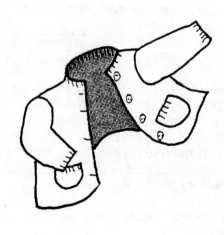

Seasonal & Holiday SPRINGBOARDS & STARTERS © EDUPRESS

Seasonal
Solutions

SPRING

- You found a small bird that fell from a nest. It's alive. What can you do?

- You are caught in a lightning and thunder storm. Where will you go for shelter?

- You picked a flower and got stung by a bee. How should you treat it?

- There is no dye with which to color the Easter eggs. What could you use?

- It's Arbor Day and you want to do something special for the environment. What could it be?

- Your friends want to play on the lawn but you are allergic to grass. What can you do?

SUMMER

- You're bored. What can you do?

- No one in your family can agree on where to go for a vacation. What is the solution?

- You're at summer camp and are very homesick. What can you do about it?

- You aren't a great swimmer but someone is daring you to go out farther in the water. What will you do?

- You need transportation to get to an important event. How could you get there?

- Your parents say you have to go to summer school. No one else is. What will you do?

Come up with a new . . .
Come up with a new . . .

*Put innovative minds to work. Choose a project;
then share the results.*

➤ *back-to-school book cover for your school*
  - create the design
  - make a sample and cover a book

➤ *kind of harvest pie*
  - list the ingredients
  - give it a name

➤ *party noise maker*
  - describe it
  - demonstrate how it sounds

➤ *snack for cold winter days*
  - write the recipe
  - draw a mouth-watering picture of it

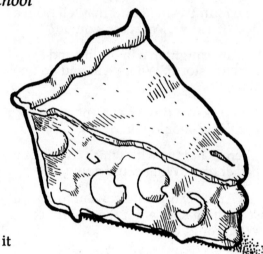

➤ *high-flying kite*
  - make a model of it
  - explain why it is different

➤ *kitchen tool*
  - describe its use
  - draw a picture of it or make a model

➤ *summer ice cream flavor*
  - write an advertisement for it
  - describe its special features

➤ *spring flower*
  - design a seed package for it
  - write a description of it

Spark comparison and observation by taking hikes together throughout the year. Talk about the changes you observed in the scenery, the homes and the activity in the neighborhood. Keep a group journal recording these observations.

TAKE a HIKE

HERE'S WHAT TO LOOK FOR:

Choose a tree to observe. Draw the changes that are seen throughout the year. How are the leaves different? What new bloom is observed? Does it have new occupants—a bird nest, tree house or insects?

How do the houses reflect the holidays? Are there jack o'lanterns on the doorstep, Christmas lights on the rooftops or other holiday symbols in the windows?

What flowers are in bloom and where are they growing?

What color changes do you observe all around?

How is the weather different on each hike?

Are the streets busier from one season to the next?

If you pass stores, how do their window decorations change? What items are they featuring for sale?

Look around your school. How are the changing seasons and upcoming holidays reflected in the classrooms?

Are bushes and trees trimmed? What changes in size and growth do you note?

Are there lawns and gardens where there previously were not?

Do you see any sign of insects or animals that were'nt present on other hikes?

Committee Concentrations

> *Divide into four groups—one for each season.*
> *Assign each group a different season but the same prompt.*
> *Collectively, share the results.*

PLAN AND PRESENT a seasonal fashion show. Write the narrative descriptions. Plan the clothing that is appropriate to the assigned season.

MAKE A LIST of seasonal safety rules.

ORGANIZE a new service-oriented group. Present the goal and decide on its first service project, appropriate for that time of year.

CREATE A TRAVEL GUIDE of good vacation destinations.

RESEARCH animal life during the assigned season.

OUTLINE a picture and create a mosaic of a seasonal symbol.

LOCATE books about or appropriate to seasonal events. Create a display.

PAINT a mural depicting the season.

INVESTIGATE an event in nature exclusive to that season. (Consider hibernation, nesting, migration, etc.)

WRITE AND PRESENT a seasonal skit.

FIND OUT ABOUT activities that are appropriate to the season in your area. Make a list of the possibilities.

ASSEMBLE weather facts for your area. What is the average temperature during that season? Other interesting facts?

CREATE a poster encouraging people to visit your community. Point out the advantages of visiting during that particular season.

> *Work in groups to make dynamic fall wall displays that feature the changes of the season in many parts of the country.*

FALL WALL

Provide each group with a strip of butcher paper, paint, scissors and glue.

Encourage them to think of the things that remind them of fall. Their challenge is to create a mural based on those associations.

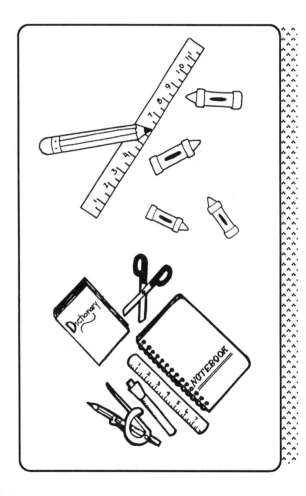

Ask students to consider, color, texture and objects.

- They may want to make a leaf mural with a background of spattered red and yellow paint.
- Their mural might be a giant football with a grassy green field painted behind.

DYNAMIC Decorations

Get groups of students involved in planning and carrying out decorating ideas for each season. Here are some basic ideas ... and some seasonal variations to add to them.

Chains and Streamers

Start with some festive paper chains and streamers.
Set aside the necessary materials in an area for "free-time" projects.

Looped chain

Cut construction paper strips that measure about 1 inch (2.54 cm) x 5 inches (12.5 cm). Decorate strips with sticky stars and glitter. Glue each strips to form interlocking loops. Alternate colors.

Braided chain

Use precut rolls of crepe paper in two different colors. The strips can be cut into any length But should be fairly long for best effects.
- Tape or staple two ends as shown.
- Fold the bottom strip of paper across the top one.
- Fold the new bottom strip over the top one again.
- Continue to fold the bottom strip over the top.

Fringed Streamer

Start with full packaged sheets of crepe paper. Cut into 2 inch (5 cm) strips.
- Don't unfold the strips from their original packaged shape.
- Make fringed cuts from both sides of the strip.
- Open carefully.
- Layer or twist two colors together.

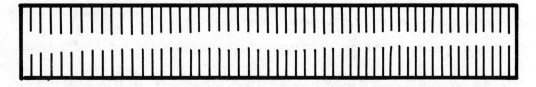

DYNAMIC
Decorations

While some groups are busy creating colorful chains and streamers to hang, others can be working on easy additions.

Winter is bright
with silver, blue and white . . .

❊ Cut snowflakes from lightweight paper. Add silver glitter.
❊ Cut icicles from aluminum foil or metallic giftwrap.
❊ Create snowmen wearing a variety of fashions.

Spring is fresh and clean
with yellow, orange and green . . .

❀ Cut several shades of green leaves. Decorate with colorful tissue blossoms.
❀ Create a variety of birds and bugs to bring the animal world to classroom walls.
❀ Cut and paste a garden of freshly bloomed flowers.

Summer is right ahead
with purple, pink and red . . .

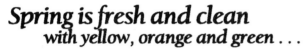

○ Make hot summer suns.
○ Sail some ships into a purple-hued sunset painted on butcher paper.
○ Hang paper beach balls from the ceiling

Fall is all around
with orange, red and brown . . .

🍂 Scatter the changing colors of fall leaves along classroom walls.
🍂 Suspend paper footballs to remind students of the sport of the season.
🍂 Harvest a field of plump pumpkins of all sizes.

Seasonal Scavenger Hunt

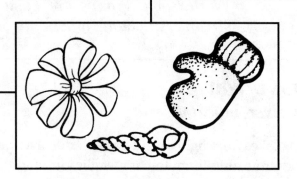

Scavenger hunts can spark learning-filled fun!

Plan a hunt for each season of the year. Just follow the steps below.

1. Give each class member a bag and a copy of the appropriate seasonal list reproduced or copied from the following page. Divide students into groups. Ask each group to brainstorm and add two original, seasonal items to their list.

2. Set a deadline of three to four days for gathering the items. All hunting must be done on student's own time, away from the classroom.

3. Allow time each day for the groups to meet and share what they've collected. They'll need to discuss, and determine which item is best for their final collection. They'll also need to update their lists and decide on the best plan for collecting the still-needed items.

4. When the allotted time is up, assemble all groups and ask them to display what they collected. Evaluate the two original items added to the list. Ask each group to explain the reasoning behind their additions.

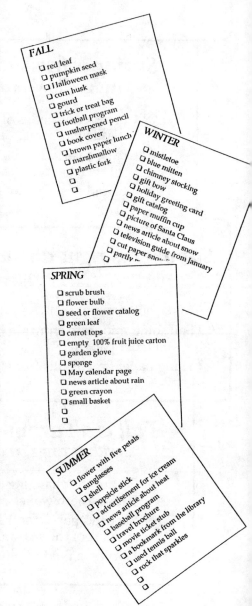

FALL
- red leaf
- pumpkin seed
- Halloween mask
- corn husk
- gourd
- trick or treat bag
- football program
- unsharpened pencil
- book cover
- brown paper lunch
- marshmallow
- plastic fork
-
-

WINTER
- mistletoe
- blue mitten
- chimney stocking
- gift bow
- holiday greeting card
- gift catalog
- paper muffin cup
- picture of Santa Claus
- news article about snow
- television guide from January
- cut paper snow
- partly

SPRING
- scrub brush
- flower bulb
- seed or flower catalog
- green leaf
- carrot tops
- empty 100% fruit juice carton
- garden glove
- sponge
- May calendar page
- news article about rain
- green crayon
- small basket
-
-

SUMMER
- flower with five petals
- sunglasses
- shell
- popsicle stick
- advertisement for ice cream
- news article about heat
- baseball program
- travel brochure
- movie ticket stub
- a bookmark from the library
- used tennis ball
- rock that sparkles
-
-

Seasonal Scavenger Hunt

Instructions on previous page

FALL

- ❏ red leaf
- ❏ pumpkin seed
- ❏ Halloween mask
- ❏ corn husk
- ❏ gourd
- ❏ trick or treat bag
- ❏ football program
- ❏ unsharpened pencil
- ❏ book cover
- ❏ brown paper lunch bag
- ❏ marshmallow
- ❏ plastic fork
- ❏
- ❏

WINTER

- ❏ mistletoe
- ❏ blue mitten
- ❏ chimney stocking
- ❏ gift bow
- ❏ holiday greeting card
- ❏ gift catalog
- ❏ paper muffin cup
- ❏ picture of Santa Claus
- ❏ news article about snow
- ❏ television guide from January
- ❏ cut paper snowflake
- ❏ partly melted candle
- ❏
- ❏

SPRING

- ❏ scrub brush
- ❏ flower bulb
- ❏ seed or flower catalog
- ❏ green leaf
- ❏ carrot tops
- ❏ empty 100% fruit juice carton
- ❏ garden glove
- ❏ sponge
- ❏ May calendar page
- ❏ news article about rain
- ❏ green crayon
- ❏ small basket
- ❏
- ❏

SUMMER

- ❏ flower with five petals
- ❏ sunglasses
- ❏ shell
- ❏ popsicle stick
- ❏ advertisement for ice cream
- ❏ news article about heat
- ❏ baseball program
- ❏ travel brochure
- ❏ movie ticket stub
- ❏ a bookmark from the library
- ❏ used tennis ball
- ❏ rock that sparkles
- ❏
- ❏

NUTTY Connections

If squirrels can harvest nuts then you can too … into a bounty of springboards for classroom learning.

This is a great center, too, for Autumn. Ask your librarian to research literature that includes a "nutty" theme.

PEANUT BUTTER

RESEARCH

- Find out how nuts grow.
- *A Pocketful of Goobers;* by Barbara Mitchell (gr. 2-5)

  A story about George Washington Carver's research with peanuts.

PROJECTS

- Make peanut butter to spread on crackers
- Sample different kinds of nuts. Compare shells and appearance.
- Learn to identify by shape
- Find a recipe that uses nuts . Make it together.

WRITE

- … a story about the nuttiest thing you have ever done.
- … and perform a *Nutty Play.*
- … an original recipe that includes nuts.
- … a story named after a nut.

  Filbert, the Nutty Detective

  Macadamia Nut Mystery
- a list of nut names:
  almond
  walnut
  peanut
  Brazil
  macadamia
  filbert
  …and more!

EXPERIMENTS

- Find out which kind is hardest to crack.
- Find out which nuts sink and which float.
- Conduct blindfolded taste tests. Who can identify the most.

JUST FOR FUN

- Have a nut cracking contest
- Run relay races with nuts in a spoon
- Guess how many peanuts are in a jar.
- Plan a "Going Nuts" day.

Springtime—or anytime—is a good time to learn about the world of plants.

Here are some activites to spark green thumbs.

PLANT PROJECTS

- Measure the length of leaves and stems.

- Find out the purpose of veins in leaves.

- Make leaf rubbings.

- Compare bulbs to seeds. Plant each and compare growth.

- Identify seeds and make a seed chart.

- Grow sprouts on sponges. Sprinkle seeds and keep damp.

- Take a trip to the local landscaping nursery. Ask the owner to conduct a tour.

- Examine the variety of petal shapes.

- Conduct experiments to find out what type of soil holds the most water.

- Dissect a flower. Identify and diagram the parts.

- Make a list of flower names. Research the meaning behind the name.

- Increase observation skills. Sketch still life pictures of flower and plant arrangements.

- Plant a variety of seeds. Compare their growth.

- Attempt to grow vegetables. Zucchini, spinach and radishes are easy for beginning gardeners.

- Learn about the symmetry in flower arranging. Use plastic flowers and vases and practice making your own arrangements.

Holiday Economics

Introduce your students to elementary economics by discussing how holidays have a special effect on business, jobs and consumer spending.

Use the following questions as discussion sparks.

• What jobs are created at Christmas time that are not in use for the rest of the year?

• What business or products depend on holiday sales for a majority of their sales?

• What are the most important holidays (or special days) when people buy and give gifts?

• What gifts are given most often for Mother's Day? Father's Day? Valentine's Day?

• What holidays are especially busy for candy manufacturers?

• What must supermarkets do to get ready for some holidays? What do you think they do with the unsold items they have left on their shelves? What do other types of stores do with leftover holiday items?

• What types of products are purchased in large numbers in the summertime?

• What kinds of clothing would sell the most at during different seasons?

• What business can you think of that may only be open in the summertime and close for the rest of the year? Are there any business that would be open just for a specific holiday? *(Hint: Christmas tree lots, Pumpkin Patch)*

• If YOU owned a business that depended on holiday spending, what kind of business would it be? Why?

• What is meant by the phrase "tourist dollars?" Why are these "dollars" important to business? What tourist destinations would be visited heavily during the holidays?

• Does anyone in your family have a job or business that depends greatly on holiday sales or vacationing travelers? Tell about it.

PANTOMIME TIME

Here's a list of holiday actions to choose from and add to.

It's said that actions speak louder than words! Play a pantomime game to prove it.

Ask students to act out holiday activities— no words spoken. Then ask classmates to try to identify the action.

You may want to provide a list for younger students to choose from. Discussion of holiday activities prior to pantomime would be helpful, too.

▼ decorating a tree
▼ lighting a menorah
▼ carving a pumpkin
▼ carving a turkey
▼ sailing on a stormy sea
  (as an explorer or colonist)
▼ mailing a valentine
▼ opening a Christmas (or other) card
▼ opening a present
▼ wrapping a present
▼ filling stockings hung by the chimney
▼ coming down a chimney
▼ playing with a dreidel
▼ baking holiday cookies
▼ shooting Cupid's arrow
▼ throwing confetti
▼ lighting—and eating—birthday cake
▼ blowing up a balloon
▼ bunny hiding eggs
▼ reindeer pulling sleigh
▼ elves making toys
▼ putting on a costume
▼ trying on new Easter bonnets

▼ watching a fireworks display
▼ raising a flag
▼ marching in a parade
▼ carolling
▼ blowing a noisemaker
▼ groundhog checking the weather
▼ shopping for a gift
▼ hanging a wreath on a door
▼ putting lights on a house

HOLIDAY ROLE PLAYING

Spark oral language and creative thinking. Take on the role of a holiday-related person or object. Be creative. Be persuasive. Have a debate. Use role playing as a springboard for writing quotations and character development.

➡ **Start with these ideas.** Encourage student pairs to develop their own role playing situations to present to classmates.

Make a telephone call to grandma and give her your ideas for a Thanksgiving meal menu.

Get on board the Mayflower and share your reaction to seeing America for the first time.

Recreate the table conversation between a Pilgrim and an Indian at the first Thanksgiving.

How did the turkey persuade the cook to fix something else for Thanksgiving dinner?

What sounds did the ghost make while trying to haunt a house?

How did the witch persuade the black cat to ride her broomstick?

Recreate the conversation between two scarecrows in a pumpkin patch.

Take the side of a pumpkin or a jack 'o lantern in a Halloween debate over which of them is more useful.

What did the Halloween costume say to the child who smeared chocolate candy all over it?

Share your conversation with Santa Claus about your holiday wishes.

How did Santa persuade the reindeer to still make the Christmas Eve flight in a blizzard?

What did Mrs. Claus say to motivate the elves in the workshop?

What did the child say to Santa when he/she found him stuck in the chimney?

What did the candle say to the birthday cake?

> **Play the part of a piece of chocolate candy describing its benefits to a dieter.**

HOLIDAY ROLE PLAYING

Recreate the conversation between Cupid and her career counselor.

How did the shy boy tell the popular girl he was a secret admirer?

What did the Valentine's Day card say to the mail carrier when delivered to the wrong house?

Share the conversation between Cupid and her arrow when selecting a target.

Persuade George Washington, Abraham Lincoln or Queen Victoria (Canada) to become your teacher.

Share the reaction of your country's flag when dropped on the ground by a member of a flag honor guard.

Take on the roles of a king or queen and an elected president debating which is a better leader.

> **Share the reaction of two leprechauns upon finding the end of the rainbow.**

Persuade the parade marshall to let you ride on your city's St. Patrick's Day float.

Take the side of an Easter Bunny or a stuffed bunny in a debate over which one makes a better pet.

Convince your father that you should be allowed to spend spring break at a friend's house.

Share your reaction to a friend who played a mean April Fool's Day trick on you.

Recreate the debate about safety between a fire fighter and a fireworks manufacturer.

You're a noise maker with a headache. Your role playing partner is a party-goer at midnight on New Year's Eve. Convince the party-goer not to use you.

> **How did the hidden egg reveal its whereabouts to the child hunting for it?**

You're a ground hog. Have a conversation with your shadow.

Role play a thankful citizen speaking to a veteran about his or her role in the military.

Great Beginnings

Every holiday has a story to tell. The story is about how it began.

Choose a holiday and find out its "story" Include tthe information that is asked below.

Be prepared to give a short history to the other members of the class.

Name of Holiday

_____

In what country was this holiday first celebrated? Around what year (or century?)

_____

_____

What person or religious reason is there for the celebration?

_____

_____

Other interesting facts:

_____

_____

_____

What symbols are associated with this holiday? How did that begin?

_____

_____

_____

Traditions observed during this holiday:

_____

_____

Quick Questions

Start with a "quick question." Discuss the various resources students can use to help them find the answer. Expand knowledge by challenging them to complete and appropriate learning extender below each question.

What is a menorah?

1. Draw a picture of one.
2. Explain what the seven branches stand for.
3. Make a model out of clay. Fill it with candles and share it with classmates.
4. Report on its importance in the celebration of Hanukkah.
5. Write an acrostic using the letters.

What is the North Pole?

1. Locate its location on a globe.
2. Research the first expedition to the North Pole.
3. Find out how the terms longitude and latitude relate to the North Pole.
4. Draw a picture of Santa Claus' home in the North Pole.
5. Describe the environment there. What are the weather conditions?

What is a reindeer?

1. Compare the differences between reindeer and other other deer?
2. Write a physical description. Include four.
3. List three ways that reindeer help the people living in Arctic regions.
4. Located areas on a map where reindeer can be found.

What is a leprechaun?

1. Make a list of other words that refer to fairies.
2. Find out about a legend associated with leprechauns.
3. Paint a portrait of this imaginary elf.
4. Find a book about leprechauns—fiction or non-fiction—and share it with classmates.
5. Write a descriptive paragraph.

Where is Plymouth Rock?

1. Find out the story behind it.
2. Make a plaster model.
3. Find its location on a map.
4. Research its history.
5. Dress as a pilgrim and explain the rock's importance to your fellow "colonists".

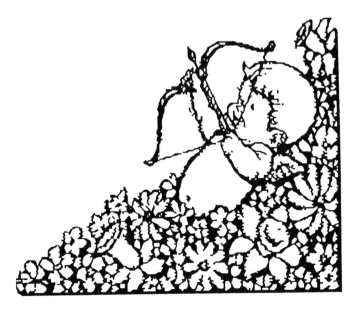

Who is Cupid?

1. Write about the legend behind Cupid's arrow?
2. Who was Cupid in Roman mythology?
3. Draw a picture of what Cupid is supposed to look like.

The sound of bells is a familiar part of many holidays.

Some research and exploration into bells will give new meaning to their holiday chiming.

Bell Ringers

Look up the definition of *bell*. What is a *clapper*? How does a bell ring and make a sound? How is the sound produced by a large bell different than the sound produced by a small bell?

Create a display of different types and sizes of bells: dinner bells, Christmas bells, bells on toys, musical bells. How are sounds produced? How are the sounds different?

How are bells made? What materials are commonly used? Discuss metals, molds and casts in the process of making bells.

What are *chimes* and *carillons:* Visit a local church or city building that chimes bells on a scheduled basis. Ask how that schedule varies with holidays.

Select holiday records or audio tapes to play. Listen for the sound of bells or the word *bells*. Clap your hands each time you hear either.

Learn carols that are named after bells: Jingle Bells, Silver Bells. Challenge students to find others.

Be **Book Bell Ringers**. Suspend a length of yarn on the wall. Provide copies of the book report bell pattern. (following) Students complete the information, color the bell and add it to the yarn.

Research famous bells and their association with holidays throughout the world. Start with the Liberty Bell, the most famous bell in America. Travel to other cities— London, England—Dolores, Mexico—Beijing, China.

Book Bell Ringers

Book Title:

Author:

Bell Rating:
(Scale of 1 - 10 bells, 10 being best)

Summary:

Holidays ... In General
Literature & Writing Sparks

Greeting card composition can provide a variety of writing experiences for holidays— and other special events—throughout the year.

Reproduce the template on the following page and keep a stack on hand for immediate prompts. Once students know how to fold and make a greeting card they can create for all occasions—or whenever the mood strikes them.

Keep a stack of greeting cards on hand for message ideas and to cut apart to create card covers.

Template instructions ...

1. Fold in half on the shortest horizontal line.
2. Fold the left side over the right.
3. Follow the paragraphs indicating where to cut and paste covers and messages.

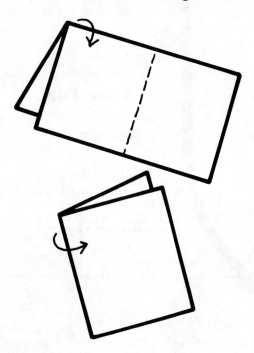

Teach values with...

- Get Well cards for class members or school staff
- Thank you notes for a class-related activity or individual students creation—at any time.
- Sympathy cards for school staff or class members who have suffered a loss.
- "I'm Sorry" messages to patch up student or family quarrels.

Teach poetry ...

- Write messages in *tanka* — a 31 syllable poem written in five lines. Rhyming is optional.

    Lines 1 and 3 each have five syllables.
    Lines 2, 4 and 5 each have seven syllables.

    Example:
    Having a birthday?
    Hope it's a real special day.
    Celebrate with friends;
    Candles, presents and cake, too.
    Make it wonderful like you.

- Assign three words. Messages must include them.
    For example— *bright, friend, thankful*
    "The world is a brighter place because
        you are my friend and I am thankful "

    "I'm thankful for knowing such a bright friend. "

Teach partner cooperation ...

- One person creates the cover. The other writes the message
- Write riddle cards. One person starts the riddle on the cover. The second finishes the riddle inside the card.

Type your message here. *(printed upside-down)*

fold line

fold line

Draw or paste your picture
in this box.

Rewrite familiar fairy tales with a holiday twist.

Fairy Tales with a Twist

Students can work individually or in small groups to rewrite familiar fairy tales with some intriguing changes. You may want to begin by reading the literature selection prior to rewriting the story.

Students may also choose to present their newly written version in a cooperative puppet show or short skit.

Here are some titles to spark creativity:

Snow White and the Seven Snowmen
Jack and the Fireworks
Sleeping Cupid
Cinder-Elf
Beauty and the Leprechaun
Santas New Clothes
Little Pilgrim Riding Hood
The Princess and the Egg

All-Purpose WRITING

Get going with holiday-related writing.

What's New With Holidays?

• Write about a holiday tradition that you think should be changed.

• If there were a holiday to celebrate kids, this is what it should be like ...

• A famous person who should have a holiday in his/her honor ...

• If _____ could be a flavor, it

   would be _____.

Fill in the blanks with a holiday name and a flavor such as mint, vanilla, maple etc. Explain the reason for the choice.

Traditional Thoughts

• My Favorite Holiday

• A special family holiday tradition or memory ...

• The person I would most like to give a gift to...

• The kind of holiday I like best ...

Mixed-up Holidays

Here are some holiday mix ups. Just imagine the results then write about them.

   • A leprechaun who delivers Christmas gifts
   • A ghost delivering Valentines
   • Cupid filling Easter baskets
   • The Easter bunny planning a gift for each night of Hanukkah
   • A Witch filling the Christmas stockings
   • St. Patrick planning a Thanksgiving feast

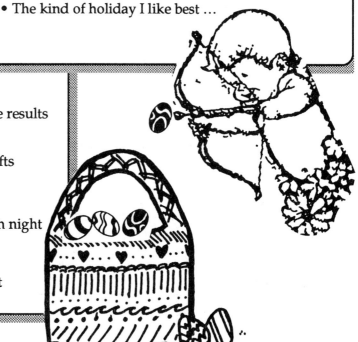

Holiday Haiku

Each *haiku* verse consists of 5 lines. The first line has just one word. Each line, thereafter, follows the pattern of increasing, then decreasing, words per line.

Word
word word
word word word
word word
word

• The first line states the subject of the verse.
• The next three lines express feeling about or description of the subject.
• The last line is a single word, again descriptive of the subject.

Here are some *holiday haiku* examples.

> *Try your hand at **Haiku** — a centuries-old form of Japanese verse.*

Ornament
Glass, glitter
Sparkling tree trimmer.
Shiny, bright
Decoration

Egg
Pastel, delicate
Filling tiny baskets.
Colorful, boiled
Hidden

Originally, *haiku* consisted of 17 syllables. The verses above have 18. Students can practice counting syllables to see how close their haiku verses can come to 17.

Once students have learned the pattern of *haiku* verse, they can write them for any—or all— holidays. You might even create a display of *haiku* verses that children can add to year-round. Put each verse inside a coordinating holiday or seasonal shape.

Some other good subjects for holiday haiku include:

pumpkin
turkey
wreath
mask
costume
ghost
cupid
Santa Claus
snowflake
valentine

Use holiday images to write limericks with your class.

These five-line poems tell a story, with first, second and last lines rhyming. Third and fourth lines rhyme independently. Read the examples aloud first so everyone has the rhythm.

There are also some first line starters to spark limerick writing. Follow up by illustrating the limericks. Read the limericks aloud and try to match it with an illustration.

Lively Limericks

Red Rudolph was pulling the sleigh.
Christmas was well on its way.
His nose got so cold,
Or so we are told
That the journey took one extra day.

A roving young Cupid from Hobart.
Shot an arrow as sharp as a dart.
It hit not a soul
But a lonely old mole.
And a romance with owl did it start.

Limerick Starters

• An elf from the town of Wazoo ...

• A leprechaun, quite sight unseen ...

• Fat Santa was donning his suit ...

• A bag full of Halloween treats ...

• A bunny with bright colored eggs ...

• A turkey without any feathers ...

• A giant white ghost with a cough ...

• A ground hog asleep in its hole ...

Spark paragraph writing with facts about the holidays. Provide each student with a copy of this page. Ask them to rewrite each set of holiday facts in paragraph form. A topic sentence is included to get writing off the ground.

Holiday History

Halloween

- Celebrated on October 31.
- Another name is All Hallow's Eve.
- Celebrations began around 700 B.C.
- Celebrations began in Wales, Scotland and Ireland.
- The Druids, ancient priests, gave banquets for ghosts or spirits living in their homes.
- The villagers dressed in costumes to "trick" the spirits into leaving town.
- Jack-o' lanterns are named after Jack O'Grady.
- He tried to trick the devil and had to carry a pumpkin lantern for he rest of his life.
- The lantern could be seen only on Halloween.

Opening sentence:

Halloween celebrations date back to 700 B.C.

Hanukkah

- The holiday lasts for eight days.
- Its name means *dedication*.
- It is celebrated by the Jewish people.
- The celebration begins on the 25th day of the Hebrew month of *Kislev*.
- It is usually in the month of December. The date is different each year.
- The Jews burned holy lamps for eight days with just a little bit of oil.
- They were celebrating a victory in a three year battle with the Syrians.
- Gifts are exchanged and contributions made to the poor.
- **Opening sentence:**

  Hanukkah lasts for eight days.

St. Patricks Day

- Celebrated in honor of the patron saint of Ireland, St. Patrick.
- He was important to the Irish because he brought Christianity to Ireland.
- His death was on March 17, 461 A.D.
- St. Patrick used the shamrock to show a religious idea.
- Celebrated in America since colonial times.
- Green worn in honor of the isle of Ireland.
- March 17 is also the feast day of St. Patrick.
- It is a national holiday in Ireland, too.

Opening sentence:

St. Patrick's day honors the death of the patron saint of Ireland.

Valentines Day

- Celebrated on February 14.
- There are many different thoughts on how it started.
- Birds choose their mates on February 14.
- St. Valentine was a saint of the early Christian church. He secretly married young couples.
- St. Valentine died on February 14, 269 A.D.
- Pope Gelasius named February 14 as St. Valentine's Day.
- There are many Valentine's Day customs.
- Many people send cards and gifts to their sweethearts and friends.

Opening sentence:

Valentine's Day is celebrated on February 14.

Sentence Starters

Read the sentence spark aloud. Encourage attentive listening by reading the sentence only two times. Give students a couple minutes to write a sentence in response. Share your sentences by inviting a student to write theirs on the board. Punctuate, capitalize and check spelling together.

Write a sentence ...

... using the colors red and green

... telling what Santa says to Mrs. Claus befor leaving on Christmas Eve

... telling what you would say if you saw a ghost

... with three spooky Halloween sounds in it

... that tells what Rudolph would say to a doctor after getting his nose fixed

... describing what you would put on top of a Christmas tree

... about an exciting gift

... with one of the reindeer's names in it

... about a problem the Easter Bunny had

... starting with the word furry

... about Valentine's Day that makes you giggle

...telling what you would say to the President of the United States or the Prime Minister of Canada

... telling what the sign over Cupid's front door says

... describing an elf in Santa's workshop

... with three Easter basket contents

... that tells what a jack o' lantern said after it was lit

... telling how a pumpkin feels about being carved

If I saw a ghost I would tell him he wasn't so scary, after all!

Just for fun ...

Choose one of the sentences to illustrate. Everyone can illustrate the same one and compare the results or choose different ones and write the sentence with a caption underneath.

Something Old
Something New

Here are some fun sparks to get kids thinking creatively. Whenever possible, ask them to find out about the "old" way then come up with something new and original.

DESIGN

- A fashionable new hat for a witch
- A new suit for Santa Claus
- A uniform for Cupid
- A new form of transportation for Santa Claus
- Giftwrap for the holiday of your choice
- Something new to send on Valentine's Day
- Something new for the Easter Bunny to hide

RENAME

- Santa's reindeer
- Columbus' three ships
- The holiday of your choice
- The place where Santa Claus makes his home
- A carved pumpkin
- The colonists who celebrated the first Thanksgving

CREATE

- A turkey-less menu for Thanksgiving
- A unique vegetable to be carved into a jack o'lantern
- Something to throw on New Year's Eve (other than confetti)
- A new phrase to say instead of "trick-or-treat"
- Five non-edible items to be handed out on Halloween
- Something safe for Cupid to shoot
- A new shape for a shamrock

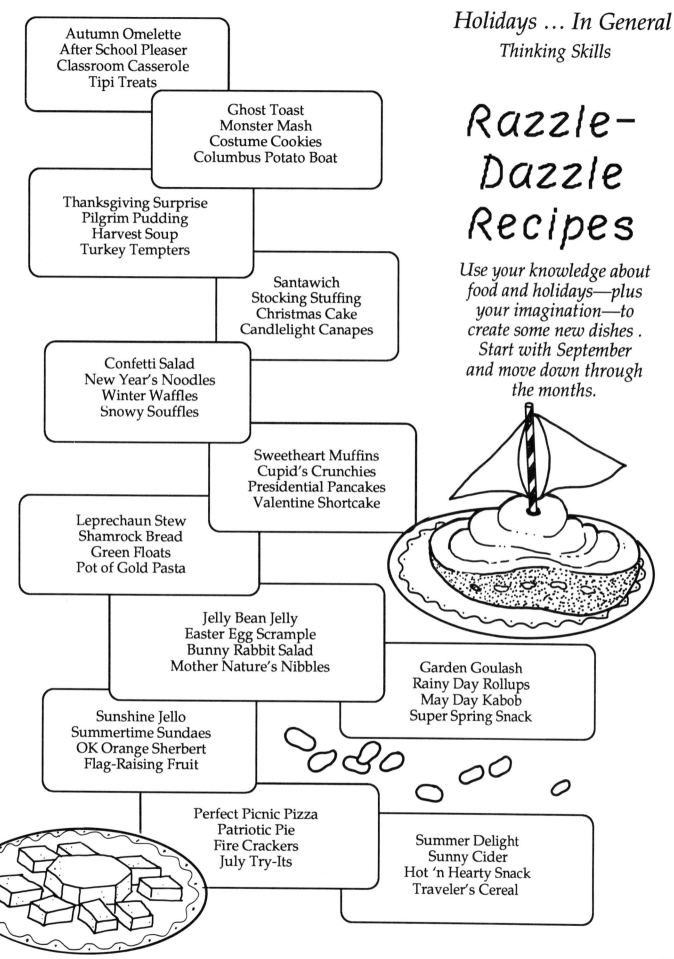

Autumn Omelette
After School Pleaser
Classroom Casserole
Tipi Treats

Ghost Toast
Monster Mash
Costume Cookies
Columbus Potato Boat

Thanksgiving Surprise
Pilgrim Pudding
Harvest Soup
Turkey Tempters

Santawich
Stocking Stuffing
Christmas Cake
Candlelight Canapes

Confetti Salad
New Year's Noodles
Winter Waffles
Snowy Souffles

Sweetheart Muffins
Cupid's Crunchies
Presidential Pancakes
Valentine Shortcake

Leprechaun Stew
Shamrock Bread
Green Floats
Pot of Gold Pasta

Jelly Bean Jelly
Easter Egg Scramble
Bunny Rabbit Salad
Mother Nature's Nibbles

Garden Goulash
Rainy Day Rollups
May Day Kabob
Super Spring Snack

Sunshine Jello
Summertime Sundaes
OK Orange Sherbert
Flag-Raising Fruit

Perfect Picnic Pizza
Patriotic Pie
Fire Crackers
July Try-Its

Summer Delight
Sunny Cider
Hot 'n Hearty Snack
Traveler's Cereal

Razzle-Dazzle Recipes

Use your knowledge about food and holidays—plus your imagination—to create some new dishes. Start with September and move down through the months.

ANIMAL ACTIVITIES

Animals are often a featured part of holiday celebrations. Make them featured members of classoom holiday activities, too. Here are some ideas:

Animal Associations

Different animals are associated with many of our holidays. Reindeer remind us of Christmas. Dragons make us think of Chinese New Year. Rabbits hop into our mind when Easter is mentioned. Make a chart of other animals associated with holidays and the roles they play in the celebrations.

New Associations

There are still many holidays without a special animal. Make an animal part of another holiday. Tell why that animal was chosen and how it would be incorporated into that holiday's celebration and traditions.

Animal Celebrations

If animals celebrated a holiday, what would it be called? Why would they celebrate it? What would they do? Write an "press release" that describes the holiday events. For example:

PEANUT DAY
Celebrated worldwide by elephants. Dinner consists of peanut butter and jelly sandwiches, roasted peanuts and peanutty pie. There are peanut tossing contests and a parade of peanuts.

Fashion Animals

Choose an animal to paint and dress in a holiday outfit. Think about these possibilities:
- A giraffe in an Easter Bonnet
- A leopard in stars and stripes.
- A lion in a Halloween costume.
- A hippopotamus in Santa's suit.
- A gorilla in Pilgrim attire
- A zebra in explorer's clothing

Develop observation, recall and application skills by observing changes in these holiday-related activities.

Encourage students to describe the look and feel of objects before and after change takes place.

Responses can be shared in in the form of group discussion or descriptive writing.

BEFORE and AFTER

Columbus Day
- soak a piece of wood in water
- blow a fan into a tub of water
- look at an object through binoculars

Halloween
- melt a chocolate candy bar
- carve a pumpkin
- fry pumpkin seeds

Thanksgiving
- husk an ear of corn
- bake a pie crust
- peel an orange

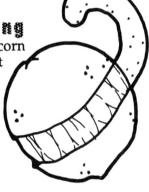

Hanukkah
- burn a new candle
- peel a potato
- spin a top

Christmas
- plug in a string of lights
- Make a bow from a length of ribbon
- stuff a stocking

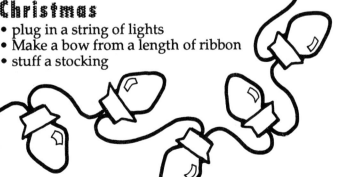

New Year's
- blow on a noisemaker
- cut paper into confetti
- compare January's calendar page to last year's

Ground Hog Day
- dig a hole in the ground
- use a flashlight to make hand shadows
- view the classroom from ground level

Valentine's Day
- seal an envelope
- put your hand over your heart and run in place
- put a marshmallow in a cup of hot chocolate

Easter
- peel a boiled egg
- sprout grass seeds
- soak a dry sponge in colored water

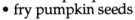

It's Time to Play …
Holiday Jeopardy

Play this adaptation of the television game show for a change of pace. Explain the format of the game. Practice giving an answer and then coming up with the correct question.

Carefully read the instructions below for game hints.

Review the following three pages.

• **The first** consists of answers to read to the students. This is the script for the emcee.
• **The second** consists of the correct responses.
• **The third** is a blank page to reproduce for students to use for written responses.

Review the preparation for playing.

• Select one student who will be the assistant emcee to select the category and point value. (Points are used in this version as opposed to money.)
• Reproduce and distribute a blank grid to each student.

Review the playing rules.

• The student emcee selects a category and point value. The teacher reads the answer. Students have a given amount of time (20-30 seconds) to write their response in the correct space on their grid.
• Mark each answer on the emcee's grid as it is read to avoid repeating the answer.
• At the end of reading all answers, collect student response sheets and check them. A maximum score is 900 points. Correct spelling is not important.
• Award prizes or treats to the top winners and to all participants.

Think of other ways to play classroom jeopardy.

• Make up your own answers to current curriculum studies.
• Create an oral version of this adapted version.
• Play with three players as in the television version.

Seasonal & Holiday SPRINGBOARDS & STARTERS © EDUPRESS

HOLIDAY JEOPARDY

	COLORS	CUSTOMS	WORDS	NAMES OF HOLIDAYS	DATES	FOODS
10 POINTS	red and green	Trees are decorated for this celebration.	Going from door-to-door dressed in costumes.	This holiday started with a discovery on October 12, 1492.	The date of Martin Luther King Jr.'s birthday.	A treat with red and white stripes and bent at one end.
20 POINTS	black and orange	Costumes and masks are wo for this holiday.	A 3-leafed plant that is a symbol for a green day.	A holiday celebrated on the 4th Thursday in November.	Halloween, the spookiest of all holidays.	These are boiled, colored and hidden.
30 POINTS	green	Lacy cards, candy and flowers are given on this day.	The word used for a holiday when all federal offices are closed.	A leprechaun is a common symbol for this day.	January 1st, every year.	A berry served with Thanksgiving dinner.
40 POINTS	red, white and blue	Fireworks are a traditional display on this holiday.	Another word for the Festival of Lights.	This holiday honors workers.	Special love is expressed on this date every year.	Sweets that come in heart-shaped red boxes.
50 POINTS	pink and red	People get pinched for wearing a certain color on this day.	The name of a holiday honoring two men in U.S. history.	The Fourth of July is the common name for this holiday.	The second Sunday in May, honoring women.	The most common bird served on Thinksgiving.

Answer sheet to read to jeopardy players.

HOLIDAY JEOPARDY

	FOODS	DATES	NAMES OF HOLIDAYS	WORDS	CUSTOMS	COLORS
10 POINTS	What are candy canes?	What is January 15?	What is Columbus Day?	What is "Trick or Treat"?	What is Christmas?	What colors are used for Christmas?
20 POINTS	What are Easter eggs?	What is October 31?	What is Thanksgiving?	What is a shamrock?	What is Halloween?	What colors are used for Halloween?
30 POINTS	What are cranberries?	What is New Year's Day,	What is St. Patrick's Day?	What is a legal holiday?	What is Valentine's Day?	What color is worn on St. Patrick's Day?
40 POINTS	What are chocolate candies?	What is February 14?	What is Labor Day?	What is Chanukah?	What is July 4th (or Independence Day)?	What color celebrates a national holiday?
50 POINTS	What is a turkey?	What is Mother's Day?	What is Independence Day?	What is President's Day?	What is St. Patrick's Day?	What colors are used on Valentine's Day?

Correct Question Response Sheet

FOODS	DATES	NAMES OF HOLIDAYS	WORDS	CUSTOMS	COLORS
10 POINTS					
20 POINTS					
30 POINTS					
40 POINTS					
50 POINTS					

HOLIDAY JEOPARDY

Response Sheet

Remember to write your response in the form of a question!

Top Score Possible: 900 points

Name:

My Score

Birthday Bash

Help your country celebrate its birthday by working cooperatively to plan and carry out a party in its honor.

Bake a Cake

Design a spectacular **paper** cake. Cut, paste, and decorate it with patriotic frosting and candles.

Find out how many candles should be on the cake. Make that number of paper candles and display them on the wall.

Write a description of the cake you "baked." What type of cake is it? What flavor is the frosting? What kinds of trim and decoration does it have on it?

Plan a Parade

Plan a parade route. Post a map of the route along with the time of the parade. Invite other classes to come and watch your parade. Show them where to sit "along the parade route". Be sure to assign some class members to be in charge of "crowd control". What other jobs need to be filled to help run the parade more smoothly?

Design a simple float. Decorate wagons or bicycles with patriotic colors and symbols.

Create a banner or mural to head the parade.

Decide on an order for the parade. Floats first? Create a list showing the order.

Locate some good, patriotic marching music to play in the background.

Dress in patriotic colors. Make patriotic placards to carry.

Be Creative

Design placemats, napkin and paper plates. Transfer your designs to paper napkins and plates. Inexpensive plain paper placemats can be purchased at a party supply store. Be sure the design reflects a historical event in your country's history.

Blow up balloons—and measure their circumference while you're at it!

"Shop" for a special birthday gift. What would you like to give to your country? Make a cooperative photo essay of these carefully selected gifts.

Create an oversized birthday card for your country. Write a poetic verse.

Assemble birthday <u>BIG BOOKS</u>. Write about the gifts your country has given you. Then put them inside one big decorated birthday cake shape.

Decorate the classroom with national symbols. Discuss their meaning. If you live in Canada, find out why the maple leaf appears on the flag. If you live in the United States, find out why the eagle is a national symbol.

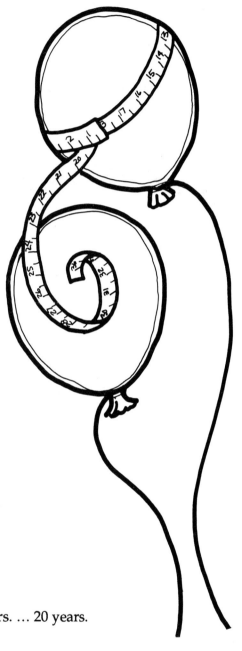

Be a Fact Finder

Find out
- What year your country was "born".

- How many years old it will be in ten years. … 20 years.

- Who is the "father" of your country.

- How it celebrated its first birthday.

Birthday Bash

What to do with
RED
WHITE
and BLUE

Engage your class in creative activities to celebrate and honor patriotic holidays and major events such as the Olympics and national elections.

Divide the class into five groups. Assign each group a different type of poetic form such as haiku, cinquian, couplet, tanka or free verse. Each student in the group writes an individual poem; then each group presents their color poems to the rest of the class on a separate day. Display finished work or assemble into a class book on holiday poetry.

For an election day in an election year, get students involved in the process and stage a mock victory party. Hold a class election for the candidates the day before election day and count ballots. Involve students in decorating your room with red, white and blue streamers, banners and placards to honor the victorious candidate.

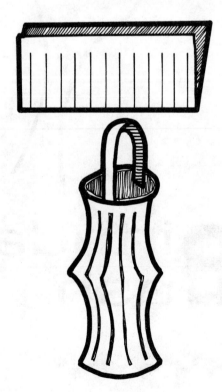

Make red, white and blue lanterns to string across the room.

Fold a piece of construciton paper in half lengthwise.

Cut slits from the folded edge to within 1/2 inch (1.25 cm) of the open edge. Open and turn to form a lantern.

Staple top and bottom. Add a paper handle for hanging the lantern.

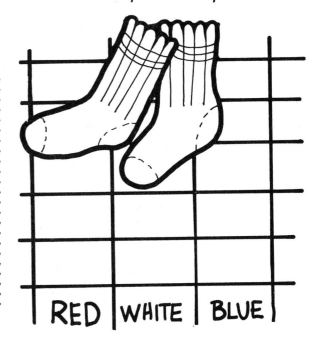

Have students dress in red, white and blue on a given day. Graph what the children are wearing.
- Red, white or blue socks?
- Red, white or blue skirts or slacks?
- Red, white or blue shirts or blouses?
- Red, white or blue jackets?

Tally the results and compare. Create math problems from the graph for students to answer aloud.

RED | WHITE | BLUE

Invite parents to make red, white and blue treats such as cupcakes decorated with white frosting and red hots. Or serve crackers spread with cream cheese and boysenberry jam.

Divide students into groups of three or four students and have them make red, white and blue *windsocks*.

- Use a tagboard strip to form the circle frame at the top.
- Hang strips of crepe paper from the top.
- Attach string to each side of the cardboard circle and hang the windsock near the windows where the breeze will gently blow them.

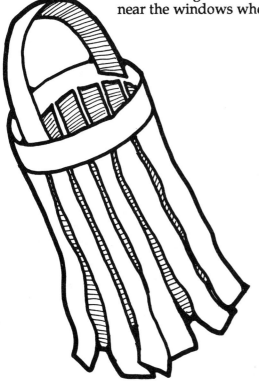

What to do with
RED
WHITE
and BLUE

Quick Gifts

Here are some ideas for easy gifts to make. Just adapt them to any holiday or event where a thoughtful student-made gift is in order.

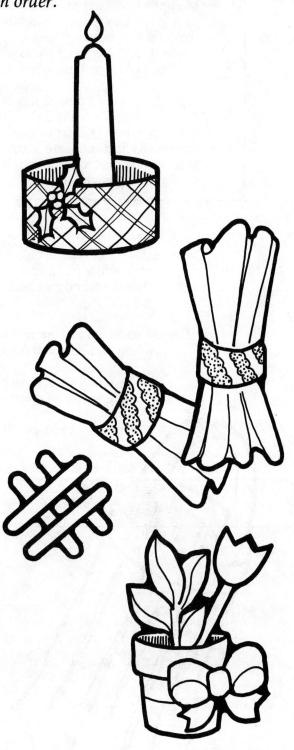

Candle Holder

Cover a small tin can (tuna fish size) with paper to suit the holiday. Try red for Christmas and Valentine's Day, orange for Thanksgiving and blue for Hanukkah.

Glue a bottle top, edges up, into the bottom of the can.

Decorate the can with trims—holiday symbols, holly or fall leaves, trims.

Floral clay will hold a candle in place in the bottle top.

Napkin Rings

Sponge paint paper tubing with holiday colors. Cut into rings approximately 2 inches (5 cm) wide. Fill each napkin ring with a colorful paper napkin before wrapping.

Tabletop Trivet

Start with four popsicle or craft sticks. Glue two sicks over the other two as shown in the illustration.

Allow the glue to dry. Paint the finished project with tempera or enamel paint. Spray with a clear lacquer.

Plant Ornament

Cut a tulip shape from cardboard. Paint.

Glue the tulip to the end of tongue depressor or craft stick.

Plant small seedlings. Insert the ornament in the soil before tying a ribbon around.

Quick Gifts

These gifts are also appropriate for year-round gift giving. These add a personal touch—fond memories of a child growing up.

Hand Memory

Work in pairs to complete this project.

Dip string in a bowl of glue. The glue may be tinted with tempera paint. When the string is saturated pull it out using the thumb and index finger to remove some of the excess glue.

One child lays a hand flat on waxed paper.

The partner outlines the hand with the string.

When outlining is complete, carefully lift the hand. Allow the glue to dry then remove the waxed paper.

Mount the stiffened yarn to paper. Make a note of the child's age.

Photo Holder

Cut two paper circles about 4 inches (10cm) in diameter. Scallop one circle and cut a hole in the center.

Glue the circles together with student picture inserted between.

Me Scroll

Supply each student with a strip of butcher paper.

Have students add personalized touches—footprint, hand print, lock of hair, lip prints, photograph, illustration or painting, etc. You may even mark student's height to create a growth chart.

Encourage students to write a special poem or note to the gift's recipient.

Be sure to include the date and student's name.

Stationery Sparks

Special paper makes creative writing more inviting ... and the results more eye-appealing. Why not ask students to be stationery designers?

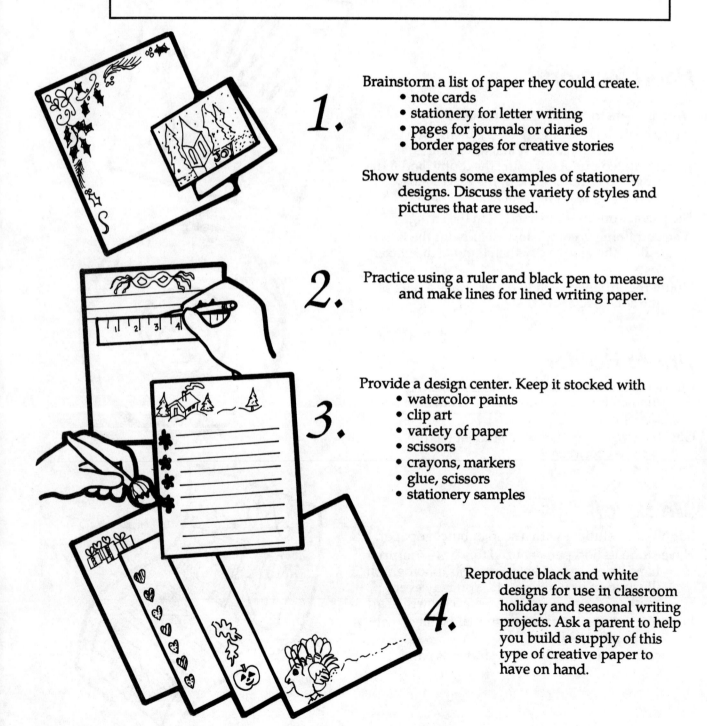

1. Brainstorm a list of paper they could create.
- note cards
- stationery for letter writing
- pages for journals or diaries
- border pages for creative stories

Show students some examples of stationery designs. Discuss the variety of styles and pictures that are used.

2. Practice using a ruler and black pen to measure and make lines for lined writing paper.

3. Provide a design center. Keep it stocked with
- watercolor paints
- clip art
- variety of paper
- scissors
- crayons, markers
- glue, scissors
- stationery samples

4. Reproduce black and white designs for use in classroom holiday and seasonal writing projects. Ask a parent to help you build a supply of this type of creative paper to have on hand.

RECYCLING for Fun

Don't throw away that holiday trash. Turn it into springboards for class projects. Encourage students to be on the lookout, too, for ways to recycle. Invite them to plan and organize project and activity using recycled holiday goods.

Here are some suggestions to get students started.

Gift Bows

- Tack in rows for bulletin board borders.
- Use as calendar markers.
- Compile a related vocabulary list—
  curl, wrap, wind, decorative
- Glue to paper to create a colorful collage.
- Take apart and measure ribbon length.
- Take apart and design originals.

Greeting Cards

- Cut off fronts to use as postcards.
- Use fronts as creative writing sparks.
- Read verses aloud for expression.
- Use verses for choral reading
- Use verses as examples for poetry sparks.
- Cut apart for gift plaque decoupage.

Candles

- Conduct melting experiments,
  then use melted wax to—
  - create original paintings
  - seal class letters and envelopes
  - illustrate vocabulary—
    swirl, contrast, blend

Gift Boxes

- Use large boxes to "house" creative writing stories—
  Cover lid as gift. Write about the surprise gift inside.
  Paste a story inside box.
- Decorate and use as desk organizers.
- Use for classroom cupboard storage.
- Use as student paper organizers.
- Collect assorted sizes formeasurement activities.
- Fill with smaller boxes for area concept activities.
- Stack for size comparisons.

Open-Ended HOLIDAY ART

Start with a group of art and craft materials. Offer no directions. Invite students to create whatever they want—using any or all of the supplies provided, plus scissors and glue when needed.

Halloween

- orange & black tempera
- pumpkin seeds
- straws
- waxed paper
- toothpicks

Thanksgiving

- yarn
- magazines
- crayons
- dried corn husks
- earth tone construction paper

Christmas

- red & green tissue paper
- tinsel, gummed stars
- colored pencils
- ribbon
- Christmas stencils

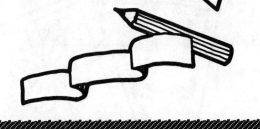

New Year

- confetti
- felt markers
- sponges
- glitter
- tempera paint

Valentine's Day

- construction paper
- watercolors
- giftwrap
- sequins
- lace

Easter

- colored cellophane
- crushed egg shells
- fabric scraps
- cotton balls
- crayons

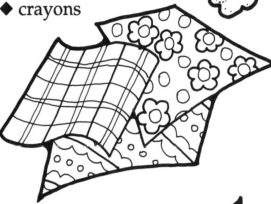

Earth Day

- paper plates
- dried beans
- tissue paper
- leaves
- clay

May Day

- construction paper
- popsicle sticks
- tempera paint
- crepe paper
- ribbon

PAINT
PINK

Open-Ended
HOLIDAY ART

Find out more about Christopher Columbus and the impact he made on history with his famous voyage in 1492.

Columbus Crusade

Roleplay Columbus asking the Queen of Spain for money to finance his voyage.
Make a poster advertising Columbus' voyage and recruiting sailors for the trip
Build a cardboard and paper model of one of Columbus' ships.
Explore other voyages made by Columbus.
Chart the route the ships travelled to America

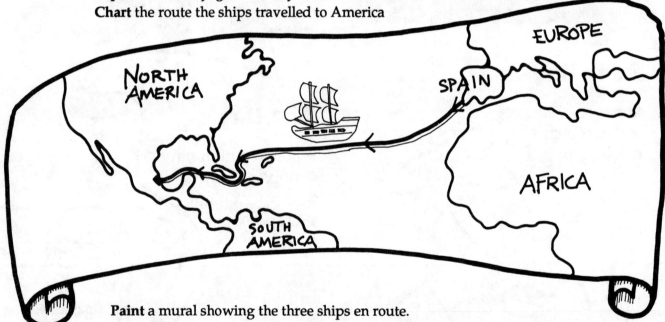

Paint a mural showing the three ships en route.
Brainstorm a list of Columbus' related words. Write them on a banner under the heading VOYAGE VOCABULARY
Research the life of Columbus. Write as many facts as can be assembled.
Prepare for the voyage to America. Divide into groups to do some planning. If you were Columbus, what would you need on the ships?
Find out what existed in North America before the arrival of Columbus.
Write a paragraph from Native American point of view about the arrival of Columbus.
Research some new discoveries about Columbus that were made during the time of the 500th anniversary of his 1492 voyage.
Draw a shape of the world; then try to draw it flat.
Imagine that the world is flat. What kinds of problems would that create?

United Nations Day

United Nations Day is October 24. It commemorates the date in 1945 that the required number of nations signed the United Nations Charter, officially establishing the United Nations (UN).
He are some prompts for increasing awareness of this global organization on its day of recognition.

Choose from these hand-on projects.

※ Create a display of newspaper articles relating to UN activity.

※ Draw a picture of the United Nations flag. Write a paragraph about what it symbolizes. (See above). The map of the world is surrounded by olive branches that symbolize peace.

※ Write a poem about friendship and brotherhood.

※ Plan a Halloween service project for UNICEF.

※ Ask each student to draw a picture of people helping other people. Put them together to make a large brotherhood quilt.

Write these questions on a large strip of butcher paper. Challenge groups of studentsto find and write the answers underneath each question.

※ What does **UNICEF** stand for.?
   (United Nations Children's Fund)

※ How many nations belong to the organization?
   (155)

※ Where are the UN headquarters?
   (New York)

※ What are the two main goals of the UN?
   (peace and harmony)

※ On what date was the UN established?
   (October 24, 1945)

※ List 10 countries that are members of the UN.

※ What is the constitution of the UN called?
   (The Charter of the United Nations)

※ What is the main body of the UN called?
   (The General Assembly)

※ Who was the first president of the General Assembly and what country was he from?
   (Paul-Henri Spaak/Belgium)

※ What UN group is in charge of keeping the peace?
   (The Security Council)

※ Who is your country's representative to the UN?
   (Answers will vary)

A Canadian Thanksgiving

Thanksgiving Day in Canada is celebrated in much the same way as it is in the United States. It is a day for a harvest celebration, family feasting and giving thanks.

The second Monday in October is reserved for this holiday.

Harvest Celebration

- Have a corn-husking contest
- Ask students to visit a grocery store with their parents and make a list of fresh fruits and vegetables currently being harvested and offered in the produce department. Together, compile a class list then make a mural collage reflecting the season's harvest.
- Use corn husks and pumpkin seed to create an original art project.

Family Feasting

- **Prepare** a classroom "feast" for special invited guests—or just class members.
  - Include a fresh vegetable tray offering current crops.
  - Serve freshly popped popcorn
  - Paint pumpkins with fall-colored designs to use as centerpieces.

- Select a Thanksgiving story to read aloud. Suggestion:
  One Terrific Thanksgiving by Marjorie Sharmat.
  A bear goes frantic searching for holiday food until he learns the true meaning of Thanksgiving.

Giving Thanks

- Write a poem that gives thanks for something special in life or that recognizes the Thanksgiving celebration in some way. Start by reading
  Merrily Comes Our Harvest In: Poems for Thanksgiving by Lee Bennett Hopkins. This collection of 20 poems dealing with Thanksgiving should lend a spark.
- Make category lists of things you are thankful, and not so thankful for. Include: food, personal habits, things to do, world situations and things found in your community. Use pictures or words to express your thoughts.

Thankful for

Not Thankful for

CITIZENSHIP SAVVY

Citizenship Day is celebrated each year on September 17. The day honors native-born citizens who have reached voting age and naturalized foreign-born citizens. Spend the day considering the privileges and responsibilities of citizenship.

CITIZENSHIP STARTS

- Find out the voting age in your country. Calculate how many years it will be before you can vote.
- Stage an election for class officers, complete with secret ballot. Encourage everyone to vote.
- Discuss the responsibilities that every citizen has to neighborhood, community and country.
- Find out how someone becomes a citizen of your country.

RESPONSIBLE DECISIONS

- Work together to create a list of classroom responsibilities for good citizens. Consider such things as caring for your school community , honoring your country's flag, voting in a class or school election and accepting responsibility for your actions

  Make a large replica of your country's flag. Write the list inside the flag and display it throughout the year.

CITIZENSHIP RECOGNITION

- Reward every student during the day with a note that recognizes the way in which they make a positive contribution to the class. Invite students to help with this. Find a good-citizen quality in everyone … Consider attitude, sportsmanship, teamwork and effort.

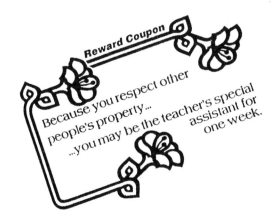

Reward Coupon

Because you respect other people's property... ...you may be the teacher's special assistant for one week.

HALLOWEEN HAUNT

Share the excitement of Halloween with these spooktacular multicurricular activities.

Decorate your school. Disguise a door. Brew clever decor for the library or office. Convert the cafeteria into a haunted house.

Make bookmarks decorated with Halloween symbols. Pick spooky books to read.

Create a costume box. Ask everyone to contribute silly hats, masks and costume discards from home. Use the costumes for
• story starters • roleplaying • character development

Recycle shopping bags by turning them into creative trick-or-treat bags.

Paint a mural showing what the <u>sounds</u> of Halloween might **look** like.

Tape a recording of student-created Halloween sounds.

Describe what a well-dressed witch might wear.

Write a story about a runaway pumpkin.

Write 4-line pumpkin poems. Display them in a pumpkin patch of yarn and leaves.

Estimate the number of seeds in a pumpkin.
Carve and count.

Conduct a "Guess the weight of the pumpkin" contest.

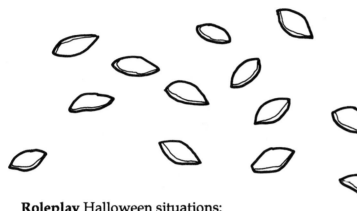

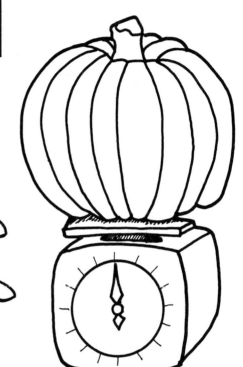

Roleplay Halloween situations:
  • a witch training her black cat
  • a ghost trying to haunt a house
  • a jack o'lantern coming to life

Develop a new, Halloween comic strip character.

Explore superstitions—Have a debate, brainstorm a list, discover the origins.

Disguise a paper pumpkin with an imaginative costume made from construction paper and material scraps.

Discuss wise rules for observing Halloween safety.

Design safety posters to display around school and the community.

Problem-solve these Halloween dilemmas:
  • Pumpkins are on strike. They refuse to be picked. What will everyone do for a jack o'lantern?
  • You are a ghosts that wears only NEON pink! You're can't be seen but neon **does** stand out. What do you do?
  • A bully is trying to steal your trick-or-treat bag on Halloween night. What will you do?
  • Everyone is scared of the monster. He is lonely. What can be done to help?

Holiday Menu
Halloween

Study spiders.
- Write descriptive paragraphs
- Make a list of interesting facts.
- Make stuffed mobiles
- Challenge students to memorize 30 different names.
- Make an insect/spider comparison chart.
- Test the strength of a spider's web.
- Find out how a spider spins its web.
- Find out what other homes a spider constructs.
- Write spider word problems to develop math facts.

Use the eight legs as the multiplier and divider. For example. There were 64 legs counted in the spider web. How many spiders were there?

Something's different this year—the official colors of Halloween are red and green instead of orange and black. Paint a picture that shows how Halloween looks in its new colors.

Write a four-line Halloween rhyme. Alternate lines written in black and orange.

Create some unusual recipes. Try Wicked Witch's Soup, Ghost Toast or Goulish Gourd Pie. Use measurment terms to write the recipe.

Create a Witch's Pantry study center. Invite students to design labels for empty cans and boxes and stack them on shelves in the center. For more advanced study, ask them to list nutritional content on labels. Some pantry content ideas:

- Cream of Black Bat Soup
- Dem Bones
- Skeleton Sausage Balls
- Clanking Crab Legs

Start a social studies investigation. Find out about real ghost towns. What does the term mean when referring to a town. What causes the boom—and the bust? Analyze … Could your city or town ever become a "ghost town"? Why or why not?

HALLOWEEN HAUNT

LITERATURE LINKS

Here are literature titles to share on this holiday. Each title is followed by a short summary and followup activity.

Sir William and the Pumpkin Monster
by Margery Cuyler (2-3)
In this turnabout story, it is the ghost who gets the scare.

Start with a pumpkin pattern. Use construction paper scraps to turn it into a monster.
• Write stories with unusual plot twists.

Halloween ABC by Eve Merriam (gr. 3-6).
An alphabet book with an older-student twist … A is for wormy, squirmy apples.

Assign student pairs to develop an imaginative Halloween alphabet using adjectives to describe each letter's subject.

The Thirteen Day of Halloween
by Carol Greene (gr. 1-5).
A Halloween-oriented spoof on the classic Christmas carol.

Work in cooperative groups to develop a part of a large classroom mural with originalthings in different categories for each number.

Spooky Riddles by Marc Brown (gr. 2-6)
Fully illustrated riddles.

Follow the format in the book to write and illustrate your own Halloween riddles. Be imaginative. Great for all ages.

The Halloween Tree by Ray Bradbury (gr. 5-6).
Boys visit a deserted house and find a pumpkin tree.

Rewrite the story with a tree that bears a different Halloween object
… a black bat tree … a broomstick tree … a ghost tree …

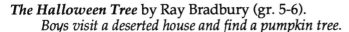

Thanksgiving Thoughts

Give students the opportunity to use multicurricular skills for these Thanksgiving related questions and projects.

❦ Math

❦ Ask each student to go to the supermarket and write down the weight of six different packaged turkeys. Total the weights to find the average weight. What is the weight of the largest turkey? the smallest?

❦ Look through grocery store ads:
   • Write down current prices per pound (or kilo) for the following Thanksgiving menu items: sweet potatoes or yams, fresh cranberries, whole pumpkin.

   •Comparison shop. Which is more expensive ... fresh, whole cranberries or the equivalent weight in a canned version?

   • Establish a budget for your Thanksgiving dinner. Make a shopping list. Calculate the costs and stick within the budget. Discuss the results. Was it easy or difficult to stay within the budget?

❦ If each student invited all aunts, uncles and cousins to their house on Thanksgiving Day, how many people would be there, including their own family members?

❦ When is Thanksgiving Day officially held in the United States? On what date will Thanksgiving fall this year? Find out the dates of the last three Thanksgivings. Find out the dates of the next three Thanksgivings. Do you see any pattern?

❦ How many years ago was the first Thanksgiving dinner held? Research the date and form the subtraction problem to arrive at the answer.

❦ Prepare a pumpkin pie in class. Measure the ingredients.

❦ Calculate the total weight of turkey that would be eaten if every student in class consumed a 12 pound turkey ... an 18 pound turkey ... a 22 pound turkey. Calculate the metric equivalent.

❦ Write Thanksgiving word problems and share the solution process.
   Example:
   • If your family cooked a 15 pound turkey, how many pounds (or the metric equivalent) would each member have to eat to finish the turkey?

❦ *Social Studies*

❦ Find out about life in the colonies. What were the hardships faced by the early settlers? What were their successes?

❦ Make a map of the 13 colonies. Put a star by the one where the first Thanksgiving dinner was held.

❦ Who were the *Pilgrims*? Who shared Thanksgiving dinner with them?

❦ Find out what foods were introduced to the colonists by Native Americans.

❦ Compare Thanksgiving celebrations and traditions of today with those of the original colonists.

❦ Pretend that you are journalists. Write headlines that might have appeared in the colonial newspaper *The Daily Pilgrim*. Here are some ideas to get you started:

New Food Discovered

Illness Strikes Colonies

Town Meeting Held

Work in pairs to write an accompanying article. Remember the basics of good reporting ... **who, what, when, where and why.**

❦ Do some role playing. Pretend you are a reporter and interview some of the guests at the first Thanksgiving dinner.

❦ You are a photographer for *The Daily Pilgrim*. Draw a picture of your most famous photograph.

Thanksgiving Thoughts

Thanksgiving Thoughts

❦ *Language and Literature*

❦ What is something that happened to your family this year for which you are grateful?

❦ Write from the points of view of a colonist:
- You are on a ship, leaving England and sailing to America. What is life like aboard the ship?
- What are your thoughts when you finally see land?
- Why did you decide to leave England?
- What was your first day like in your new home? Write an entry in your diary.

❦ Make a list of foods that are harvested during Thanksgiving.

❦ Dramatize a scene from the first Thanksgiving or a harvest festival.

❦ Create and write a Thanksgiving menu using students' choice of food. Encourage use of creativ[e] lettering and descriptive food words for each foo[d] item.

❦ Design placemats and invitations for a holiday feast

❦ Think of another appropriate one-word name for th[e] holiday instead of Thanksgiving.

❦ Describe a memorable Thanksgiving you shared wi[th] family or friends.

❦ Read holiday recipes. Rewrite them without looking at the original. How much did you remember?

❦ Write a shopping list for a trip to the grocery store in preparation for Thanksgiving dinner.

❦ Find out about and report on the relationship between the Indians and the colonists.

❦ Brainstorm individual lists of things students are thankful for. Compare the similarities and differences between the lists.

Thanksgiving Thoughts

Literature Links

Here are literature titles to share on this holiday. Each title is followed by a short summary and followup activity.

❦ *Cranberry Thanksgiving* by Harry and Wende Devlin. (all grades)
Grandmother suspects that someone stole her famous cranberry bread recipe.

Use the recipe in the book, or find your own, and bake a batch of cranberry—or other—bread.

❦ *Molly's Pilgrim* by Barbara Cohen (gr. 2-4)
A Jewish immigrant girl find acceptance in her third grade class when her mother makes a clothespin doll at Thanksgiving time.

Create Pilgrim, or other dolls, out of clothespins.

❦ *Thanksgiving at the Tappletons* by Eileen Spinelli (gr. 2-3).
Just because there isn't turkey and trimmings doesn't mean the family gives up on their holiday dinner.

Plan an unusual Thanksgiving or harvest meal. Illustrate the new, creative menu.

❦ *Thanksgiving Day* by Robert Merrill Bartlett (gr. 2-5)
An introduction to the harvest festival in Canada and Thanksgiving in America.

Paint large pictures of harvested fruits and vegetables such as pumpkins, squash and corn. Cut them out and assemble in one large mural.

❦ *The First Thanksgiving* by Joan Anderson (gr. 2-5).
A recreation of life with the Pilgrims from the Mayflower to the first Thanksgiving.

Write and present a short skit depicting the events in the book.

Veteran's Day

On November 11, a legal holiday, the people in the United States set aside the day to honor those men and women who have served and died in military service to their country.

The observance includes parades and speeches.

HONOR THE OBSERVANCE WITH THESE ACTIVTIES ...

- Invite grandparents to speak about how life and views changed during World War II

- Make a time line of the history of war in your country

- Discuss the role of the military in your country

- Make a patriotic mural

- Find out the origin of the holiday

- Find out the original name of the holiday (Armistice Day)

- Make a list of memorials

- Talk about the purpose of a memorial

- Research the Tomb of the Unknown Soldier.
  - Discuss the meaning of the inscription
  "Here rests in honored glory and American soldier known but to God".
  - Rewrite the inscription on a scroll.
  - Find out about similar memorials in other parts of the world
  - Find out about continued tradtions
  - Locate Arlington, Virginia—the location of the national cemetery—on a map

- Present short patriotic speeches

- Share any military uniforms parents may have

- Have a debate about the value of war

- Find out what leaders were in office during the wars in your country

- Compile a related vocabulary list and make look up the words in a dictionary

Include: *veteran, memorial, uniform, peace, war, unknown, remembrance, battle, military, armed forces, soldier, cemetery*

IN CANADA:

Canadians observe REMEMBRANCE DAY on November 11. The men and women who died in World War I and II are remembered on this day.

- A red poppy is the symbol. Make painting of red poppies to display in the classroom.

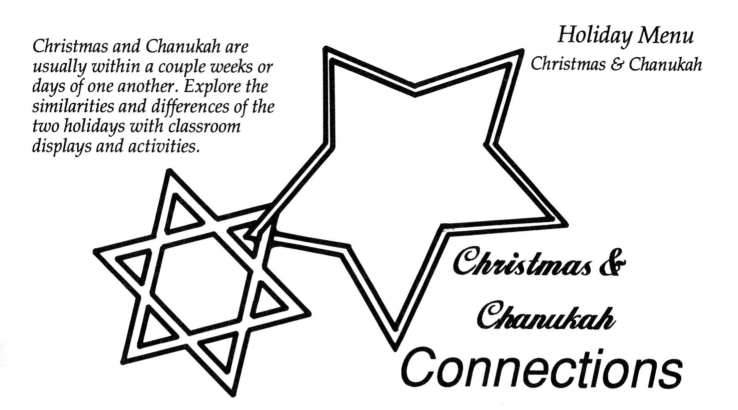

Christmas and Chanukah are usually within a couple weeks or days of one another. Explore the similarities and differences of the two holidays with classroom displays and activities.

Christmas &
Chanukah
Connections

Set up two tables next to each other. On one arrange literature that tell the story of Chanukah. Ont the other, display literature about Christmas. Take time throughout the day to choose a book from each table to read aloud. Encourage children to do the same. Compare the information and stories.

Make two charts:

Chanukah Holiday Foods	Christmas Holiday Foods

Paste pictures, recipes and menus that reflect foods that students' families traditionally eat or that are associated with each holiday.

Conduct a Holiday Spelling Bee. Select words appropriate to student level or derived from literature read aloud in class.

Listen and compare songs of Israel with songs heard at Christmas.

Divide into two groups to write and present skits that retell the story of each holiday.

Compare the symbols connected with the two holidays. Find out about the importance of the star. Make a mobile that includes the shapes of both Christmas stars and the Star of David.

Make paper or real wax candles. Discuss the role of candles during both holiday seasons.

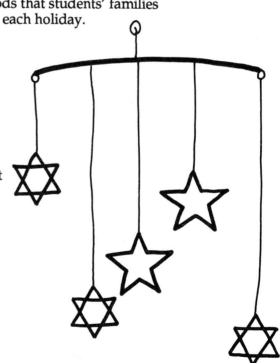

Chanukah Happenings

Each year in the month of December, Jewish people throughout the world celebrate Chanukah. Chanukah is the Hebrew word for "dedication". It's a holiday filled with eating special foods, playing pecial games, singing songs and giving and receiving gifts.

Plan a Chanukah Color Day. Dress in blue and white.

Decorate the room with white and blue streamers.

Find out when Chanukah is celebrated this year. Sometimes it comes very near the beginning of December and sometimes it is celebrated later in the month. Research the difference between the regular Gregorian calendar that we use versus the Jewish calendar.

Classroom Cookery

Prepare some *Latke*—the Yiddish word for pancake. Potato latkes are one of the most popular Chanukah foods. They're made from grated potatoes and chopped onions held together with eggs and flour then fried in oil. Find a recipe for latke in a cookbook and prepare this dish in class. Serve with applesauce.

Bake sugar cookies using the most common Chanukah shapes—an elephant, candle or the Star of David. Decorate with white frosting and blue sprinkles.

Make a chart of the various ways to spell the name of this holiday.
Hanukkah, Chanukah, Hanukah, Channukah, Hannukah, Chanukkah
These are all accepted!

Play traditional Chanukah games using a *dreidel*.

Star of David Projects

- Cut two triangles from construction paper
  Overlap and glue toghether as shown.

- Make potato stamps.
  Dip in blue paint and stamp onto white paper.

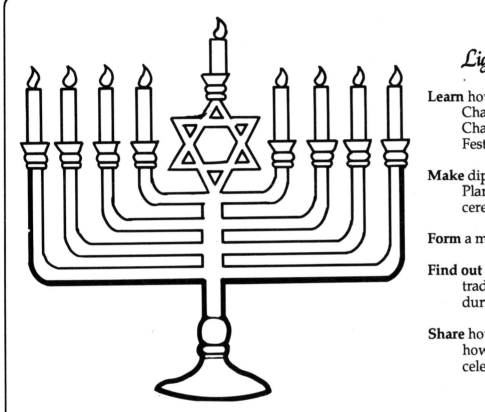

Lighting the Menorah

Learn how the menorah is lit during Chanukah. Find out why Chanukah is also called the Festival of Lights.

Make dipped wax candles together. Plan your own candle-lighting ceremony.

Form a menorah out of clay.

Find out about the gift-giving traditions that are followed during Chanukah celebrations.

Share how your family—or find out how a family you know— celebrates Chanukah.

Literature Resources

The Hanukkah Book *by Marilyn Burns. Four Winds Press.* A complete book including recipes for latkes, sugar cookies, candles, etc.

Chanukah *by Howard Greenfeld. Holt Rinehart and Winston.* A brief book describing the history of the holiday.

Chanukah Happenings

Christmas

'Round the World

Spark global awareness with 'round the world Christmas activities. Find out that people the world over are the same ... yet different.

Santa, by any other name

Children of many countries believe in Santa Claus, but most refer to him by a different name. Learn to match the name with the country.

COUNTRY	NAME
Austria	St. Nikkolo
Belgium Germany Czechoslovakia Spain Switzerland	St. Nicholas
Brazil, Peru and other parts of South America	Papa Noel
China	Shen Tan Lao Jen
Denmark	Jul emanden
Finland	Ukko
France	La Pere Noel
Holland	Sinter Klaas
Hungary	Kriss Kringle
Italy	Babbo Natale
Sweden	Julomten

Christmas

'Round the World

Traditions

🍃 Make a crown of paper candles for St. Lucia Day in **Sweden.**

🍃 Make and break a paper bag pinata for Mexico and **Latin America.**

🍃 Decorate a small tree, a tradition begun in the Black Forest in **Germany.** Sing *O'Tannenbaum.*

🍃 Make rice pudding, a dessert enjoyed at Christmas dinner in **Denmark, Norway** and **Sweden.**

🍃 Make a paper shoe. Fill it with magazine pictures of gifts. The children of **France, Spain** and the **Netherlands** put their shoes in front of the fireplace on Christmas Eve so that Father Christmas can fill them with gifts.

🍃 Role paper to resemble a yule log, the burning of which is a tradition in **Italy.**

🍃 Fill a sock with "goodies" a tradition shared by children in **Canada.**

Activities

🍃 As a whole-class cooperative project, write a play that depicts all of these worldwide Christmas traditions. Present the play in a pageant to other classes.

🍃 Challenge students to find Christmas stories from other lands to read to or share with classmates. Keep a large map handy and mark the lands represented with a pushpin.

🍃 Keep a chart of the countries whose traditions you have read about.

Spruce up your curriculum with these sparks.

Christmas Capers

Language

Stuff a stocking with vocabulary words. Pull one out each day and add a page to personal word books. Draw a picture, define, share your thoughts. Here are some words to include.
- Yule • tinsel • garland • wreath • ornament • sleigh
- workshop • stocking • chimney • decoration

Write rebus sentences using compound words. Start with
- candlelight • gift wrap • reindeer
- wonderland • workshop • wonderland

Develop sequencing skills. Give each student participating a sack of Santa's stuff—candy cane, muffin cup, small jingle bell, ornament, etc. Empty the contents of the sack. Refill the sack following oral directions. Invite students to give the directions, too. Older students may add to the complexity of the directions.

Solve these Christmas problems:
- Santa got stuck in our chimney.
- Rudolph's nose is dull instead of bright.
- The reindeer are fighting among themselves. All of them want to lead the sleigh.
- It's so foggy, the sleigh can't travel on Christmas Eve.

Writing Titles
- Elf Escapade • Miracle in Santa's Workshop
- Mrs. Claus' Surprise • Christmas Eve Traditions

Write and present a reindeer revue with reindeer puppets.

Science

Make a list of the kind of trees used for decorating. Find out about the differences between spruce, pine, and fir trees.
- Compare needles to leaves.
- Take apart a pine cone. Examine its parts.
- Conduct an experiment to find out how long a branch in water and out of water will take to dry out.
- Conduct scent tests. Can a tree be identified by its scent?

Learn to identify holly, mistletoe, poinsettia. What are the traditions connected with each?

Find out which holiday plants, if any, are poisonous.

Grow a plant in a paper cup. Tuck it inside a reindeer planter made from rolled brown construction paper. (See illustration.) Add a red paper nose and big eyes.

Snap up your senses. Sniff and identify holiday scents …
- pine   • bayberry • cinnamon • vanilla •cloves

Experiment with plants. Put a stalk of celery in a cup of water dyed with red food coloring and another in water dyed green. Observe the path of the dye as it travels up the stalk.

Math

Red Hot Math — Create and solve math problems using red hot candies as counters.

Mistletoe Measurement — Hang mistletoe with string from the ceiling. Vary the length of the string. Give students measuring tapes and ask them to record the distance from the floor to each hanging mistletoe cluster. Record measurements. Compare results.

Mural Math — Make a mural of the 12 days of Christmas. Challenge older students to do it in multiples. For example, a mural in the multiple of four would have 20 golden rings and 28 swans.

Write word problems —
- If a 6 foot tree has 6 branches for every linear foot, how many branches does it have all together? (Create metric problems, too.)
- Santa starts with 16 gifts. He puts two in each stocking. How many stockings can he fill?

Christmas Capers

Thinking Skills

Design a gift for Santa. After all, he's always giving. Now it's time for him to receive. What will you select? Why?

Find a new use for Christmas stockings instead of filling them with small gifts or stuffers.

Make a list of all the Christmas carols and songs you ever heard. Create a class list. How many different ones did you think of? How many do you know by heart?

Talk about "Christmas in July". What would it really be like if it were true? Create an imaginary summer Christmas. Sand instead of snow? Ice cream cones instead of candy canes? Bathing suits instead of winter jackets?

Art

Create an unusual tree topper ornament.

Make an easy ornament. Glue a doily to a plastic margarine tub or coffee can lid. Dot with glue and sprinkle with glitter. Poke a hole in the lid and hang with ribbon.

Design personalized stockings. Start with a basic shape. Color to suit individual interests. A ballet slipper? A soccer shoe? A tennis shoe riding a skateboard?

Turn a paper plate into two projects.
- Cut out the center. Decorate and make an ornament.
- Cover the remaining circle with torn tissue paper painted on with a mixture of glue and water. Add a red bow. Roll red tissue to create holly berries and glue to wreath, too.

Christmas Capers

Literature Links

Here are literature titles to share on this holiday. Each title is followed by a short summary and followup activity.

The Night Before Christmas by Clement Moore. (all grades)
The classic tale of Santa's Christmas Eve visit.

Assign students different phrases to illustrate.
* Retell the story by holding up the pictures in sequential order. Trade pictures and tell again.
* Present a choral reading using the pictures as props.

Arthur's Christmas Cookies by Lillian Hoban (gr.1-2).

A hilarious mix-up occurs when Arthur bakes cookies.

Share favorite Christmas cookie recipes. Compare names, ingredients. Choose one and bake a batch.

A Candle for Christmas by Jean Speare (gr. 2-4).
A Canadian tale of a Christmas promise.

Make milk carton candles.
* Conduct wax experiments. Track the melting time; Then track the hardening time. Compare.

A Certain Small Shepherd by Rebecca Caudill.
A mute boy gets an opportunity to play one of the shepherds in a Christmas pageant.

Communicate without words.
* Learn to "sing" a carol with hand signing.
* Present a Christmas play—in pantomime.

Miracle on 34th Street byValentine Davies (gr. 3-6).
An old man named Kris Kringle is hired as a department store Santa Claus.

Write letters to Santa Claus
* Address the envelope properly.
* Develop a cross-age, write-and-answer project.
* Make a collection of holiday postage stamps.

Christmas Capers

Holiday Menu
New Year's Day

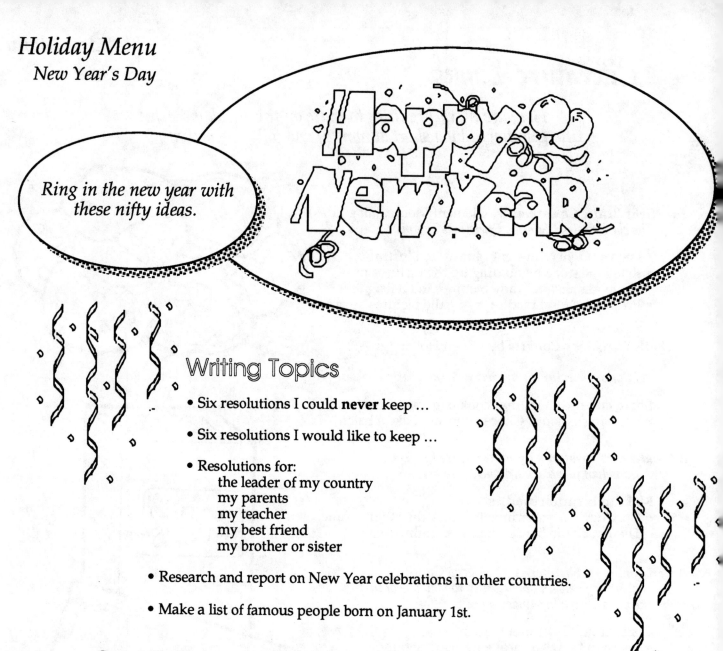

Ring in the new year with these nifty ideas.

Writing Topics

• Six resolutions I could **never** keep ...

• Six resolutions I would like to keep ...

• Resolutions for:
   the leader of my country
   my parents
   my teacher
   my best friend
   my brother or sister

• Research and report on New Year celebrations in other countries.

• Make a list of famous people born on January 1st.

Creativity

• Don't turn over an old leaf ... design one! Make it imaginative, like no other leaf in the world. Create a bulletin board with all the leaves.

• Make some imaginative calendars. Use the template on the next page to reproduce 12 pages for each student. Connect the pages with a metal brad. Add decorative trim and artwork to each page to reflect the month.

• Be a noisemaker inventor. What new sounds will we be able to use on New Year's Eve?

• Design a new party hat or colorful confetti for New Year celebrations.

• Make a banner to welcome the new year. Hang it in the school office.

• Draw a picture of the float you would design for a New Year's Day parade.

• Think of a theme for a New Year's Day parade.

sunday	monday	tuesday	wednesday	thursday	friday	saturday

BROTHERHOOD CELEBRATION

*Spend January 15, the birthday of American civil rights leader
Martin Luther King Jr., celebrating brotherhood.*

❖ Write one paragaph that describes what King accomplished in his lifetime.

❖ Write a free verse—a poem that has no set form and no rhyme pattern— that expresses the concepts of freedom, peace and racial justice that were the pleas of Martin Luther King, Jr.

❖ Find pictures of the King Memorial in Atlanta, Georgia. Discuss the purpose of a memorial. Find out what inscriptions, if any, appear on the memorial and the significance of the words.

❖ Make a brotherhood **wreath.** *(See illustration above.)* Trace and cut out hands in the colors of the human race—red, yellow, black, white, brown. Discuss the significance of the colors.

❖ Make a brotherhood **mural.** Ask each child to cut out a paper human shape in a color that represents the races of the world.

❖ Several days prior to the celebration, encourage students to find and bring to class, articles and books about King. These could be biographies or information found in reference materials. Share the stories and articles in a "freedom" display.

❖ King's birth name was *Michael.* Find out why he and his father changed both their names legally to Martin. *(In honor of the German religious leader Martin Luther.)*

❖ King's most famous speech began with the words "I have a dream …". Ask each child to contribute to a discussion with a sentence that begins with the same phrase.

Seasonal & Holiday SPRINGBOARDS & STARTERS © EDUPRESS

Chinese New Year

This Chinese celebration brings in a new year at a different time and in a different way than the traditional merriment enjoyed in the United States and Canada.

Marked by parades, fireworks and a symbolic dragon, the festivities begin on the date of the first full moon between January 21 and February 19.

* Make dragons using small milk cartons decorated with colorful, fringed tissue paper. Add a tongue and tail.

* Write stores about dragons. Start with an adjective such as fearsome, brave, cowardly or clumsy and go from there.

* Choose a book about dragons to read aloud, beginning on the first day of Chinese New Year. Suggestions:

A Book of Dragons; Hosie and Leonard Baskin. A collection of legends and myths about dragons.

World Famous Muriel and the Scary Dragon; Sue Alexander. A girl is requested to rid a kingdom of a dragon.

* Beginning January 20, track the moon's progress. Ask students to observe then draw the moon each night. Try to predict when it will be full. Check an almanac to see how close your predictions were.

* Learn about Chinese symbols. Make a border around the classroom with a symbol contributed by each class member.

* New Year parades also feature make-believe lions. Paint pictures or create paper-plate lions.

* What are the twelve animals that Chinese people name years after? What is the animal sign for this year?

* Plan a class celebration. Make lanterns and fans. Use the animal sign as a theme. Serve fortune cookies and herbal tea.

Valentine Voyages

Valentine's Day is a holiday associated with friendship, love and romance. It is a favorite of children because it involves sending and receiving cards—sometimes from secret admirers.

❤ Do some creative thinking and provide some practice with quotation usage at the same time. Ask students to come up with Valentine riddles such as:
What did the letter say to the stamp?
—"You send me!"

❤ How many funny Valentine sayings can students come up with that mention foods? Brainstorm a list of foods together then start the ball rolling with:

Lettuce be Valentines.
Peas be mine.
I'm **nuts** about you.
There's a good **raisin** to be my Valentine.

❤ Make and serve Valentine treats.
Use a heart-shaped cookie cutter
to cut mini-sandwiches from white bread
spread with cream cheese and red jelly or jam.

❤ Prepare a valentine collection box with the help of students.
- white lace paper doilies
- pink and white ribbon
- fabric scraps
- sequins and glitter
- stickers of flowers or hearts
- pastel and red tissue paper
- special fabric trims
- pieces of old costume jewelry

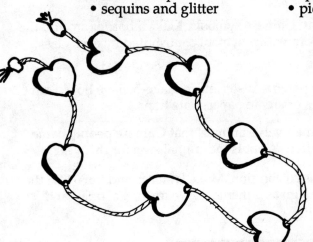

❤ Use the collection box to spark the creation of original valentine cards.

❤ Share Valentine's Day with the senior citizens of a local nursing or retirement home. Create special cards to distribute to them.

❤ Come dressed as a valentine in red, white and pink to celebrate the day.

❤ Make heart necklaces to wear.

Valentine
Voyages

❤ Have each student save 2-3 pages of their "BEST WORK" and send it home in a Valentine folder of pink, red or white construction paper decorated by the student.

❤ Share a Valentine treat with school personnel who may be overlooked ... the school nurse, psychologist, office manager, custodian, speech teacher, bus driver, etc.

❤ Keep a list of Valentine vocabulary on the chalkboard for students to use in writing activities. Alphabetize and use small illustrations for younger grades.

❤ VOTE for Valentines! After students create their Valentine cards, vote for the smallest, fanciest, funniest, reddest, etc. Be sure that each Valentine is a winner in some category!

❤ Award special heart stickers to students who say "Please" and "Thank you" on Valentine's Day without being reminded.

❤ Assign a committee of students to decorate the classroom door to look like a giant Valentine card.

❤ Create some matching heart games to share with classmates. Give each student eight medium-sized construction paper hearts. Ask them to cut the hearts in half. The cuts should be zig-zag and different on each heart. Store in zip top bags. Trade with classmates and try to match the hearts.

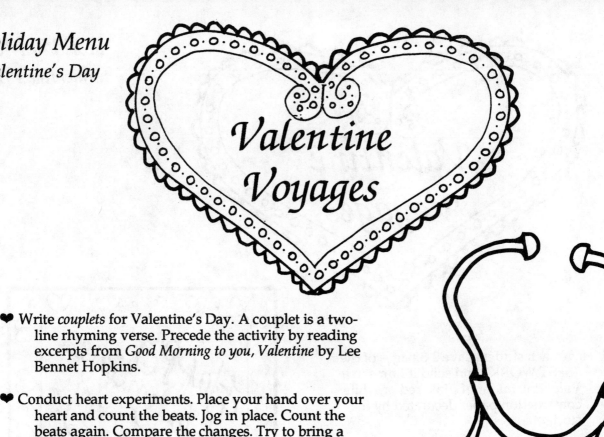

Valentine Voyages

♥ Write *couplets* for Valentine's Day. A couplet is a two-line rhyming verse. Precede the activity by reading excerpts from *Good Morning to you, Valentine* by Lee Bennet Hopkins.

♥ Conduct heart experiments. Place your hand over your heart and count the beats. Jog in place. Count the beats again. Compare the changes. Try to bring a stethoscope to class for students to listen to their heart beating.

♥ Draw and label a diagram of the human heart.

♥ Plan a "Have a Heart" service project to carry out on Valentine's Day.
  • Make cookies for the school staff.
  • Read valentine stories to younger students.
  • Write and illustrate story books for children in hospitals.
  • Make placemats or table decorations for meals delivered to the elderly and home bound.

♥ Find out about foods that are good for your heart. Make a chart.

♥ Create an area where pairs of children can go to read or study with each other.

♥ Play "Cupid". Pair up different students for the day. See what new friendships might develop.

♥ Write large numerals on hearts. Mix them up. Ask students to place them in numerical order on the chalkboard ledge.

♥ Decorate lunch bags for a special Valentine's Day picnic. Spread a big blanket and enjoy lunch together.

♥ Fill a jar with red hot candies. Ask students to estimate the number they think are in the container. Check responses and declare a winner.

Valentine Voyages

Literature Links

Here are literature titles to share on this holiday. Each title is followed by a short summary and followup activity.

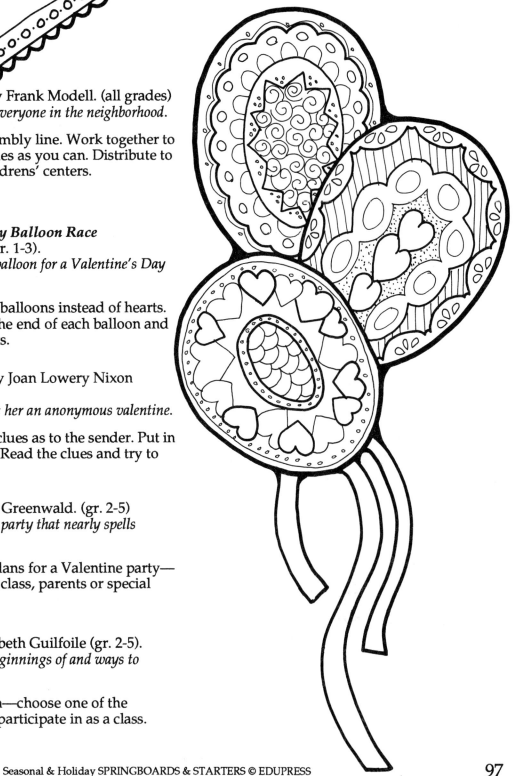

❤ ***One Zillion Valentines*** by Frank Modell. (all grades)
Valentines are made for everyone in the neighborhood.

Create a valentine assembly line. Work together to make as many valentines as you can. Distribute to local hospitals and childrens' centers.

❤ ***The Great Valentine's Day Balloon Race***
by Adrienne Adams (gr. 1-3).
Two rabbits construct a balloon for a Valentine's Day race.

Create fancy valentine balloons instead of hearts. Tie a pretty ribbon to the end of each balloon and display them in clusters.

❤ ***The Valentine Mystery*** by Joan Lowery Nixon
(gr. 2-4).
A girl finds out who sent her an anonymous valentine.

Write valentines with clues as to the sender. Put in a bag and exchange. Read the clues and try to identify the sender.

❤ ***Valentine Rosy*** by Sheila Greenwald. (gr. 2-5)
Rosy throws a Valentine party that nearly spells disaster.

Create and carry out plans for a Valentine party—for your class, another class, parents or special invited guests.

❤ ***Valentine's Day*** by Elizabeth Guilfoile (gr. 2-5).
Information about the beginnings of and ways to celebrate this day.

Make a group decision—choose one of the suggested activites to participate in as a class.

Presidential Hoopla

Presidents' Day, held on the third Monday in February, celebrates the birthdays of two American Presidents born in that month.

Learn more about George Washington and Abraham Lincoln— plus other presidents, by sparking interest with these activities.

Begin with Books & Related Activities

Who's In Charge of Lincoln? by Dale Fife (gr. 2-3)
Third grader Lincoln Farnum, named after Abraham Lincoln, ends up in Washington D.C. with a satchel of money and a wild imagination.

Get acquainted with the United States' capital through books, encyclopedias and travel guides. Make a list of the buildings and memorials found there.

Lincoln: A Photobiography by Russell Freedman (gr. 2-6)
Historical photographs, letters, posters and drawings give insight into the man who became the sixteenth president.

After viewing the photo essay, try to *write* a biography. Work cooperatively to build, sentence by sentence, a story that recreate Lincoln's life.

George Washington by Ingrid & Edgar D'Aulaire (gr. 2-4)
A simple recounting of the life of the first president of the United States.

Sharpen your writing and sequencing skills, as with Lincoln above, and work cooperatively to add sentences and "build" a biography of Washington.

Phoebe and the General by Judith Berry Griffin (gr. 2-5)
Based on a real historic incident, the story of a spy who's 13 year old daughter saves Washington from being poisoned by a member of his own bodyguard.

Find out about other Presidents who have been the victims of attempted or successful assassinations.

Presidential Hoopla

More About the Men

☆ **Have a discussion.** What do you thing Lincoln or Wahington would be most **proud** of in today's world?

☆ **What's in a nickname?** Find out why Washington is called "The Father of our Country". Why is Lincoln referred to as "Honest Abe" , "The Railsplitter" or "The Great Emancipator"?

☆ **Make a rolled paper log cabin.** Find out what life was like living in one. What would a child's responsibilities have been?

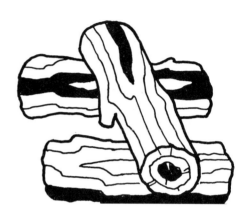

☆ **Find out** the actual birth dates of each man.

  • Lincoln, February 12, 1809.

  • Washington, February 11, 1731. **NOTE:** In 1752, America switched to the calendar used today. If that had been in use when Washington was born, his birth date would have been February 22, 1732. That is the date recognized today.

  • **Calculate** how old each man would be if he were alive.

  • **Determine** your birth date if you were born before 1752. Add eleven days to the date of your birth. If you were born between January 1 and March 25, add one year.

☆ **Retell the legend** about Washington and the cherry tree.

Other Presidential Activities

☆ **Make a graph** showing each month. Find out the birth date of every president and graph it into the correct month. Draw some conclusions from the graph data.

☆ **Find out about** the election process. Ask each student to contribute a fact. Compile a fact list.

☆ **Choose a president** and write a biography or create a time line.

It's that time of year for bunnies, baskets and eggs.

Use them as springboards for multicurricular learning themes.

Bunny Business

Prepare a classified advertisement for a new Easter Bunny. List the job qualifications. Write a job description.

Be a bunny employer. Interview a potential candidate for the job of Easter Bunny.

Debate the issue: would you rather be a chocolate bunny or a marshmallow bunny?

Write a list of nouns related to Easter.

Write a list of adjectives that would describe a bunny.

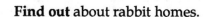

Find out about rabbit homes.

List the different kinds of rabbits. Choose one to research further.

Write an acrostic for BUNNY.

Recreate the story of Peter Rabbit. Present it as a play to younger students in a cross-age teaching program.

Find out the average age and length of a full grown rabbit.

Compare the difference between a rabbit and a hare?

Learn to do the Bunny Hop. Dance on a rainy spring day.

Write about ...
  ... why is a rabbit's foot considered lucky?
  ... How the Easter Bunny got its start
  ... Bunny Tales

Basket Tasks

❋ Bring an assortment of baskets to class. Examine the various methods in which they are made.

❋ Research the uses of baskets throughout civilization.

❋ Find out about how people have used the art of weaving to create other things that help provide basic needs. Make a chart showing the item and its uses. For example

blanket—shelter, trading, horse covering

❋ Learn how to weave dried straw or paper.

❋ Write about …

… the best thing you could ever find in an Easter basket

… the morning you found worms in your Easter basket

… The Legend of the Magic Basket

❋ Conduct some basket estimating. Line up baskets of various sizes and a supply of golf balls. Estimate how many balls it will take to fill each basket.

❋ Take a basket hike. Arm each group with a basket and ask group members to collect things such as a leaf of a particular length or a rock with a specified diameter. Brainstorm a list together.

❋ Have a food drive and fill donated baskets with food for needy families.

❋ Research the kind of designs that are painted on baskets by African-Americans and Native Americans. Recreate these designs with paint. Display them on a bulletin board.

❋ Fill a plastic berry basket with artificial grass for each student. Tuck a plastic egg inside. Encourage students to write supportive notes to each other to put inside the egg. Students will look forward to writing and reading their basket notes.

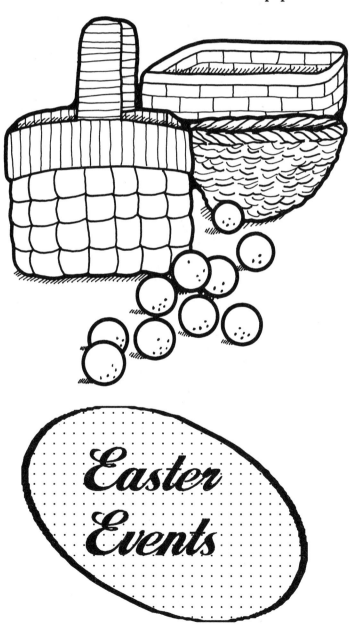

Easter Events

Egg-Ventures

Easter Events

Write paragraphs describing the different ways to prepare eggs—*boil, baste, poach, fry, devil, scramble*

Put on your thinking caps …

… an Easter without eggs? How could that be? Well, it has happened. Come up with a suitable substitute.

…Discuss the meaning of these phrases:

"Don't put all your eggs in one basket."

"Which came first, the chicken or the egg?"

"He's a good egg!"

"That really fries me."

"One bad egg spoils the whole batch."

The custom of exchanging eggs began in ancient times. The Ancient Egyptians and Persians often dyed eggs in spring colors and gave them to their friends as gifts. The Persians believed that the earth had hatched from a giant egg.

Write about a giant egg hatching. Give your own version   of what came out.

In England, friends often wrote messages and dates on the eggs they exchanged. Cut out a large egg pattern. Write a letter to a friend on it.

Find out the calcium content in an eggshell. What benefits can be derived from it?

Hide eggs. Write clues as to there whereabouts. Hunt in teams. Challenge students to hide the eggs again and write their own clues. Children may participate cooperatively.

Measure the circumference of one dozen eggs. Compare the results. What is the average size? Compare large, extra large and regular eggs. What size determines the category they are in?

Easter Events

Literature Links

Here are literature titles to share on this holiday. Each title is followed by a short summary and followup activity.

The Easter Egg Artists by Adrienne Adams (gr. 1-3).

A rabbit family paints 100 dozen eggs for Easter, helped by the son's flair for comic design.

Each class member contributes colored eggs until there are 100 for a giant bulletin board basket. Create word problems with the eggs.

The Big Bunny and the Easter Eggs
The Big Bunny and the Magic Show
by Steven Kroll (gr. 1-3).

A sick Easter Bunny must be replaced in the first title. In the second, the same bunny makes a career change.

• Draw a picture that illustrates a solution to the problem of a substitute bunny. Who will deliver the eggs … and how?
• Did the bunny make a wise decision? Discuss the decision-making process.
• Perform a magic trick for classmates.
• Talk about careers. Share your thoughts about the future.

The Talking Eggs by Robert Sans Souci (gr. 2-5).
A lesson in kindness is explored in this folk tale.

Spark a discussion about human kindness and other values. Find other folk lore to share.

The Enormous Egg by Oliver Butterworth (gr. 4-5).
An ordinary chicken hatches a dinosaur egg that gives a farm boy his own pet Triceratops.
Weird Henry Berg by Sarah Sargeant (gr. 4-6).
Another odd egg hatches, this one belonging to a large dragon.

Write chapter books about an unusual egg hatching. Work cooperatively in groups, with each submitting a chapter.

ST. PATRICK'S PARADE

It's the time of year to celebrate the green of Ireland.

THINK GREEN

♣ Create a list of things that are always green. Try to include items that are ordinary **and** unusual.

♣ The color green has disappeared this year. What color will replace it for St. Patrick's Day" What will you use in place of the shamrock? Create some new ideas for this silly situation.

♣ Plan a green treat. Then prepare and eat it. Try lime sherbert with green sprinkles or lime jello cut into shamrock shapes.

♣ Sample green vegetables such s broccoli, zucchini and cucumber. Dip them in ranch salad dressing tinted with green food coloring.

♣ Make shamrock collage using these colors:
  • kelly green   • lime green   •forest green   •emerald green

♣ Conduct a green experiment:
  Put a stalk of celery in a glass of water tinted with green food coloring. Watch what happens to the stalk over a period of time.

LEARN ABOUT IRELAND

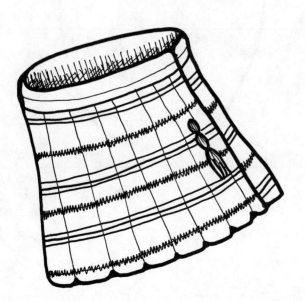

♣ Locate Ireland on a map. Find out five facts about the country. Share the facts with classmates. Make a list as the facts are shared. How many different facts were discovered?

♣ Find out why Ireland is called the **Emerald Isle**.

♣ Learn about traditional Irish clothing.

♣ When did St. Patrick arrive in Ireland?(432AD) Why is St. Patrick's Day a national holiday?

♣ Find out why the potato is important to Ireland; Then plan a baked potato buffet.

LEPRECHAUN LANGUAGE AND LITERATURE

♣ Make a list of words that start. end or contain the letter combination **SH**. Write them on a giant green shamrock.

♣ Create Shamrock **BIG BOOKS** using these story starters:

> *When I woke up my skin was green…*
> *Today I had the luck o' the Irish …*
> *The Littlest Leprechaun*

♣ Write a two-line rhyme about St. Patrick's Day. Write it in green marker or crayon. Put the rhymes together to make a long class rhyme. Is it silly or sensible?

♣ Make a St. Patrick's Day vocabulary list. Put your list in alphabetical order and create a picture dictionary.

♣ Research *Leprechauns*. Find out their place in literature. Create an imaginary leprechaun and paint a portrait of him or her.

♣ Create bag-puppet Leprechauns. Write and present a short puppet show.

LEPRECHAUN LAUGHS

♣ Learn to dance an Irish jig.

♣ Listen to a recording of bagpipe music.

♣ Participate in a shamrock hunt. Take turns hiding shamrocks in the classroom or outdoors. Practice following verbal directions by asking the hider to direct the finder to the hidden shamrock.

♣ A pig is an important symbol relating to St. Patrick's Day. Create original paper-plate pigs. Put them on a bulletin board under the heading PADDY'S PIGS

ST. PATRICK'S PARADE

Arbor Day Adventures

Arbor Day is a day set apart for planting trees. Most states in the United States and most Canadian provinces celebrate Arbor Day. The dates vary from state to state and province to province. Check your state or province for the exact date of celebration.

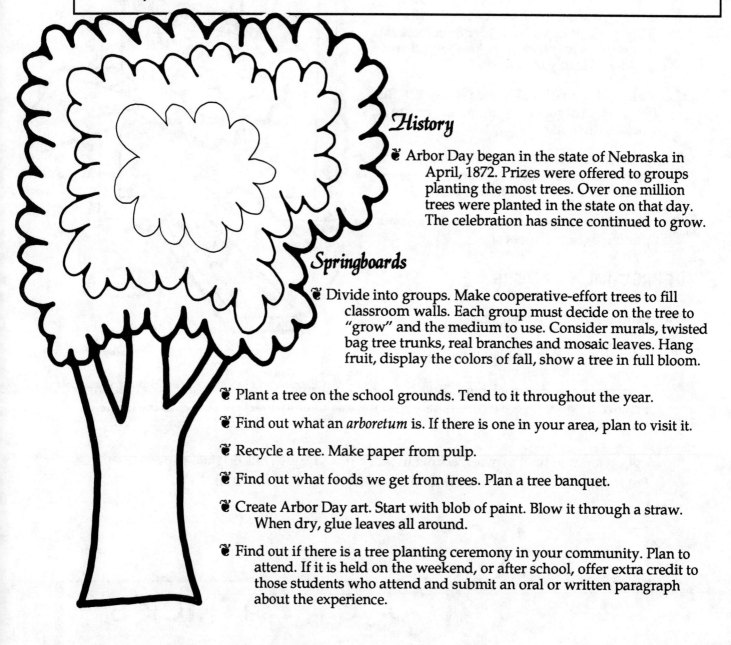

History

❦ Arbor Day began in the state of Nebraska in April, 1872. Prizes were offered to groups planting the most trees. Over one million trees were planted in the state on that day. The celebration has since continued to grow.

Springboards

❦ Divide into groups. Make cooperative-effort trees to fill classroom walls. Each group must decide on the tree to "grow" and the medium to use. Consider murals, twisted bag tree trunks, real branches and mosaic leaves. Hang fruit, display the colors of fall, show a tree in full bloom.

❦ Plant a tree on the school grounds. Tend to it throughout the year.

❦ Find out what an *arboretum* is. If there is one in your area, plan to visit it.

❦ Recycle a tree. Make paper from pulp.

❦ Find out what foods we get from trees. Plan a tree banquet.

❦ Create Arbor Day art. Start with blob of paint. Blow it through a straw. When dry, glue leaves all around.

❦ Find out if there is a tree planting ceremony in your community. Plan to attend. If it is held on the weekend, or after school, offer extra credit to those students who attend and submit an oral or written paragraph about the experience.

Here are some more Arbor Day springboards that link literature and poetry to multicurricular learning.

If these titles are not available, there are an abundance of related books available in the library. Check with your librarian for suggestions.

Literature Links

❦ *A B Cedar: An Alphabet of Trees;* George Ella Lyon. (gr. 2-6)
Contains an alphabet presentation of trees, including a silhouette drawing and hand-holding leaf and fruit samples for each.
Armed with the book, take a walk around the school's neighborhood or an area where there are trees. Try to identify the trees you see.

❦ *The Giving Tree;* Shel Silverstein. (gr. 2-5)
Little by little, a generous tree gives up everything to the boy she loves.
Discuss the meaning of friendship and sacrifice.

❦ *Oak and Company;* Richard Mabey. (gr. 2-5)
The story of an oak that lived 300 years.
• Research redwoods, the oldest living trees.
• Find out how the rings of a tree trunk indicate age.

A Poem Prompt

❦ What do we plant when we plant the tree?
We plant the ship, which will cross the sea.
We plant the mast to carry the sails;
We plant the planks to withstand the gales—
The keel, the keelson, and beam and knee;
We plant the ship when we plant the tree.

❦ What do we plant when we plant the tree?
We plant the houses for you and me.
We plant the rafters, the shingles, the floors.
We plant the studding, the lath, the doors,
The beams and siding, all parts that be;
We plant the house when we plant the tree.

❦ What do we plant when we plant the tree?
A thousand things that we daily see;
We plant the spire that out-towers the crag,
We plant the staff for our country's flag,
We plant the shade, from the hot sun free;
We plant all these when we plant the tree.

What Do We Plant?
by Henry Abbey

❦ Discuss all unknown vocabulary words.

❦ Brainstorm and make a photo essay of all the products that are made from trees. Discuss the benefits. Imagine a world without them.

❦ Divide into groups of three. Ask each member to memorize a verse of the poem. Present aloud.

❦ Present the poem as a large-group choral reading. Make a mural, backdrop or props to correlate with the reading.

May Day Magic

May 1 is a day for outdoor festivals centered around flowers and a dance around the May pole.

Although people in the United Sates and Canada recognize May Day, the biggest celebrations take place in European countries.

Here are some May Day springboards.

❀ Make small-scale May poles. Start by gluing a popsicle stick to construction paper. Provide children with recycled ribbon , a ruler or other measurement tool and a list of lengths. Measure and cut the ribbon to specifiecd lengths. Glue one end to the top of the popsicle stick and the other end to the paper.

❀ Explore the terms clockwise and counter-clockwise. Travel around an imaginary May pole in both directions. Also move in these directions: frontward, backward, forward, reverse. What other directional words can be applied?

❀ Hawaiians make flower leis to exchange as a sign of friendliness. Each May 1, a contest is held for the most unusual lei. Hold a contest in your classroom. Clean out all those scraps in your art cabinet and let imaginations run free.

❀ Research May Day customs in other countries. Compare findings.

❀ Find out more about flowers. Make a list of unusual names.

❀ Create a May Day picture. Cut a vase from recycled wallpaper or giftwrap. Paint flowers in the vase.

Taking care of our planet should be an every day event. In many areas, a special day is set aside in March or April to focus on environmental issues. Check your community for Earth Day dates and events. Use the ideas to below to spark earth-awareness activities and projects.

LEARN HOW TO MAKE a compost pile.

MAKE A LIST of things you can recycle in the classroom.

ORGANIZE a recycling program for your class. Organize one for your family. Start by turning off the lights when you aren't in a room! Report on the progress to classmates.

DISCUSS WAYS water is wasted. Brainstorm ways to conserve. Talk about such things as brushing your teeth to watering your lawn.

RESEARCH acid rain. Find out what it is , what causes it and what is being done to prevent it.

LOCATE books about or appropriate to earth day. Create a display.

PAINT a mural showing a clear sky. Now paint one showing a polluted sky.

INVESTIGATE endangered species. find out how environmental problems contribute to this status.

WRITE AND PRESENT a skit that demonstrates six ways to help save the earth.

FIND OUT ABOUT the harm that helium balloons can cause. Make a photo essay.

ADOPT a portion of your school or playground to take care of. Keep it clean. Keep it planted. Ask others to treat the area with respect. Encourage other classrooms to adopt a different area.

CREATE a newsletter that informs others of ways to save the environment. Distribute it to other classes. Have it on hand for classroom or school visitors. Send it the local newspaper for publication.

EXPERIMENT with a landfill. Bury a variety of items—balloon, string, food, styrofoam, etc. Dig it up every two weeks. Examine the decomposing rates. Draw some conclusions.

Merry Mother's Day

Remember Mom—or another special lady—with these activities.
Make a gift, write a poem, arrange something special.
Whatever the choice, the memory will be cherished!

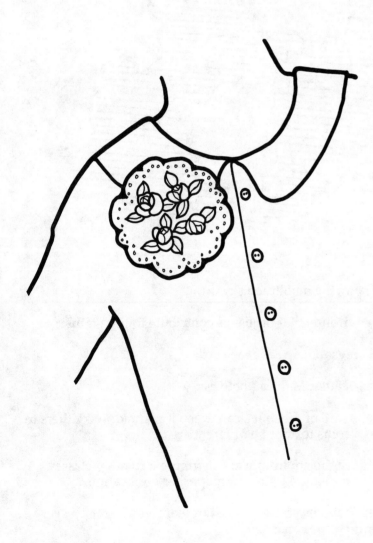

• Clip out some new recipes from magazines and arrange them in a mini-cookbook to give to your mother. Create a cover and title for your gift.

• Brainstorm a list of jobs that your mother does. Include those inside and outside the home—driving, volunteer service, cooking, cleaning, working. Compile a large class list.

• An ode is a poem that expresses enthusiasm for someone or something. Odes should be sung! Compose an ode to mothers.

• Set up a bulletin board display with pictures or photographs of

OUR MARVELOUS MOMS

Label each picture or photo with a caption such as
"My mom is a great lawyer."
"My mother bakes great cookies!"

• Design five coupons to give to your mother that she can trade in to you for certain favors or tasks. For instance, one coupon might say "This coupon good for a foot massage." "This coupon good for house vacuuming."

• Glue silk or tissue flowers and ribbon to a round paper doily. Pin the pretty doily to the dress of a special lady to wear as a corsage.

Happy Father's Day

Remember Dad—or another special man—with these activities.
Make a gift, write a story, plan to do something special.
Make this a memorable day for a memorable person.

- Brainstorm a list of jobs that your father does. Include those inside and outside the home— driving, coaching, community involvement, cleaning, working. Compile a large class list.

- Set up a bulletin board display with pictures or photographs of

  OUR FABULOUS FATHERS

  Label each picture or photo with a caption such as
  "My dad is a super golfer."
  "My father can fix anything."

- Design five coupons to give to your father that she can trade in to you for certain favors or tasks. For instance, one coupon might say
  "This coupon good for one car wash."
  "This coupon good for cleaning golf clubs."

- Interview your father. Think of six questions you would like to ask . Get to know him better. Then let him ask YOU six questions.

- Write down all the things you think are important for a father to do. Discuss your choices.

- Design an award for your father for something special he does. It can be funny or serious. For example

Sports Fanatic Award

Terrific Tool Guy

INCREDIBLE INDEPENDENCE

Independence Day celebrates the birthday of the United States, July 4, 1776.

Plan some patriotic activities to observe this occasion. Start with the sparks below.

- Write about the meaning of freedom.
- Plan a patriotic picnic then carry out the plans.
- Learn three patriotic songs and sing them to another class.
- Write a poem about your country's flag. Be sure to include stars, stripes, red, white and blue.
- Design and paint a birthday cake for your country.
- Illustrate phrases from patriotic songs.
- Create a patriotic mural.

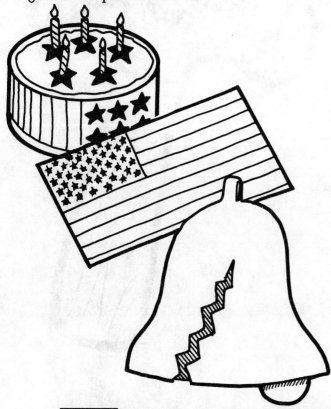

- Research the history of the American Flag.
- Make a tape recording simulating the soun d of fireworks. Make a related vocabulary list. Include explosion, boom, pop.
- Make a time line of events leading to the signing of the **Declaration of Independence**
- Take a "trip" to Philadelphia. Look through books and pictures that show historical sites.
- Read the *Declaration of Independence*. Use it as a springboard to discussion.
- Find out what the expression "Sign your John Hancock" means.
- Create firecracker art with spatter painting or by blowing a blob of paint with a straw.
- Make a paper American flag. Use it as a book cover for a story about your country.
- Calculate how many years the United States has had independence.
- Make a photo essay about the Liberty Bell or other symbol of independence.

INCREDIBLE INDEPENDENCE

Other countries also celebrate independence. Divide into cooperative groups and assign each one of the countries below.

Ask students to research the history and celebration of that country's independence celebration.

Give them the outline below as a working tool.

Canada	Dominion Day	July 1
Scotland	St. Andrews Day	November 30
France	Bastille Day	July 14
Great Britain	Boxing Day	1st workday after Xmas
Greece	Independence Day	March 25
Italy	Liberation Day	April 25

History

What important dates led to independence?

Make a timeline

What were some of the events leading to independence?

Who were the people and political groups involved?

Celebration

When was the holiday declared?

Who declared it?

What traditions are honored in the celebration?

When does the celebration take place and how long does it last?

Same Old Thing

Are you tired of hearing the same old thing?

- ***Happy** Halloween*
- ***Happy** Easter*
- ***Happy** New Year*
- ***Happy** Hanukah*
- ***Happy** Thanksgiving*
- ***Happy** Birthday*

*At least we get a little creative and say "**MERRY**" Christmas—even though it means the same thing!*

We know these are happy times of the year but let's get away from the <u>same old thing!</u>

First, rewrite each one with a new word that means **about** the same thing. Try <u>cheery</u> or <u>joyful;</u> then think of some of your own.

Rewrite each one again. This time you can choose any word you want to go in front of the holiday. You might want to try **silly** or **crazy**. At least it will be a change from the same old thing!.

Seasonal & Holiday SPRINGBOARDS & STARTERS © EDUPRESS

Just Three Words

Read each word. What does it make you think of? How does it feel? What color is it? How does it taste? What shape is it?

Write three words that describe it. Here is an example:

leaf—crunchy, green, pointed

bunny

_____

_____

_____

witch

_____

_____

_____

pumpkin

_____

_____

_____

Santa Claus

_____

_____

_____

elf

_____

_____

_____

candle

_____

_____

_____

cupcake

_____

_____

_____

snowflake

_____

_____

_____

Holiday Confusion

Something is wrong with each sentence below.

Rewrite each one and change the words or words that are wrong so that the new sentence makes holiday sense!

The jolly leprechaun filled the stockings.

_____

The bunny hid the colored shamrocks.

_____

They carved the tomato and put a light inside.

_____

I pinched him because he wasn't wearing blue on St. Patrick's Day.

_____

It was Arbor day so I played a trick on her.

_____

They lit another light bulb on the second night of Hanukkah.

_____

They heard the moose on the rooftop on Christmas Eve.

_____

The costumed children knocked on the door and said "Fill my bag."

_____

It was May Day so I gave her a bouquet of ribbons.

_____

During Hanukkah they feasted on traditional turnip pancakes.

_____

I put some shamrock-shaped candies in her Valentine card.

_____

Choose a holiday. Write the holiday you have chosen on the line below. Complete the chart using pictures or writing—or both. Choose another holiday and do the same thing with a second worksheet. You may want to do more and make a booklet to share with your classmates.

The Way I Celebrate

Special foods I enjoy with my family.	
Songs I like to sing or listen to.	
New clothes I buy or something special I wear.	
A story I like to hear or a book I've just read.	
A special tradition my family shares.	
A TV show I saw about this holiday ... and what it was about.	

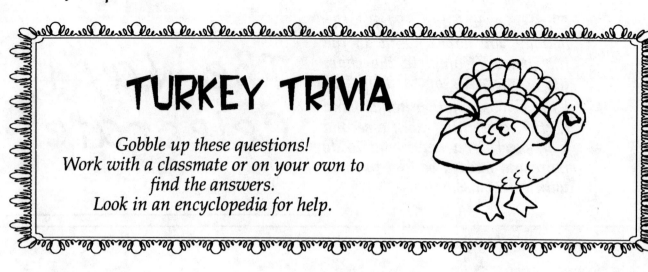

TURKEY TRIVIA

Gobble up these questions!
Work with a classmate or on your own to
find the answers.
Look in an encyclopedia for help.

1. Male turkeys are called _____. Female turkeys are called _____.

   Baby turkeys are called _____.

2. What are the two *species* of turkey? _____ _____

3. What are the differences between the wild turkey and the domestic turkey?

   _____

   _____

4. What is a wattle? _____

5. What are the three leading turkey-producing states? _____

   What is the leading turkey-producing Canadian province? _____

6. Describe one way that turkeys are like chickens and one way they are different.

   _____

   _____

7. How do wild turkeys live? _____

8. What kinds of domestic turkeys are raised commercially? _____

   _____

9. What is the sound that a turkey makes? _____

10. What are two brands of turkey sold in your local grocery store? _____

    _____

Name _____

Holiday Treats

Most holidays have special foods associated with them. Many hours are spent in kitchens creating colorful and delicious recipes and food ideas to add to a holiday feast.

Look through some magazines with recipes. Cut out a recipe created for a particular holiday. If it is illustrated or has a photograph, cut that out too.

Paste the recipe and picture below.

Put your recipe on a bulletin board alongside the recipes of classmates. Compare the variety that you found. Take a vote to see which sounds the tastiest, the most unusual and the most traditional.

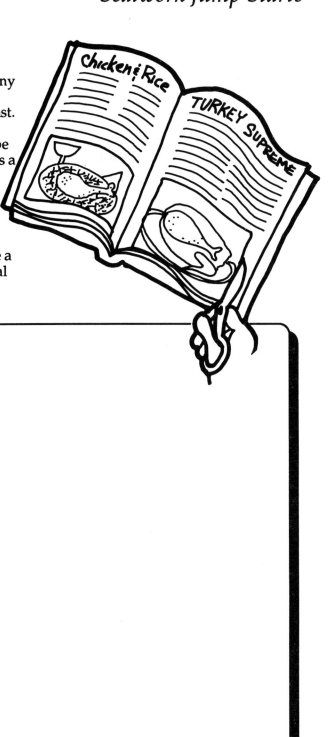

Put-togethers

Examples:

A lively leprechaun went shopping for a rainbow.

The big box was hiding the lost reindeer.

Put together a holiday sentence.

*Use a phrase from **column 1** and a phrase from **column 2**. Add as many other words as you want. Change the phrases a little if you need to.*

How many different sentences can you make? You may need more paper.

Look at the examples for ideas.

1.

were filled to the brim

couldn't find the gift wrap

decorated with a bow

gift from Santa

needed to be cleaned

stuffed with chocolate treats

lost reindeer

invited all the relatives

spent her allowance

lively leprechaun

2.

stockings on the chimney

went shopping

her lacy valentine

brand new bicycle

the big box

walked through the snow

went on a trip

looked at a map

festive holiday meal

cooked a big dinner

Holidays in the United States

How much you know about holidays in the United States? If you don't know an answer, try to find out!

President and Congress designate the holidays to be observed by federal employees throughout the country. These are called *legal* holidays.

List the legal holidays that have been set by the President and Congress. Include the name and date for each.

_____ _____

_____ _____

_____ _____

In addition to legal holidays, each state has the authority to decide other holidays it will observe. List the holidays your state observes that are in addition to the legal ones listed above.

_____ _____

_____ _____

_____ _____

What is the difference between a traditional holiday and a legal holiday?

_____

_____

_____

List three traditional holidays.

_____ _____ _____

Stocking
Sentiments

Write your thoughts about what you would stuff in the holidays stocking of the people below.

Your best friend

The President or Prime Minister of your country

a patient in a hospital

a newborn baby

a millionaire

yourself

Plan a snack for Santa.

Read the descriptive words. Think of a snack that fits that category.

Draw it or glue magazine picture that shows your choice.

Describe it in a short sentence.

A Snack for Santa

crunchy	**chewy**	**sweet**

nutritious	**spicy**	**sour**

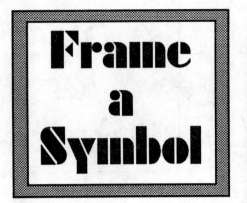

Create one large grid using yarn, ribbon or paper strips to divide the sections. Be sure there is a "frame" for each student.

Use the grid all year long and simply change the pictures with student-created paintings and cutouts of symbols and reminders representative of the holiday or season at hand.

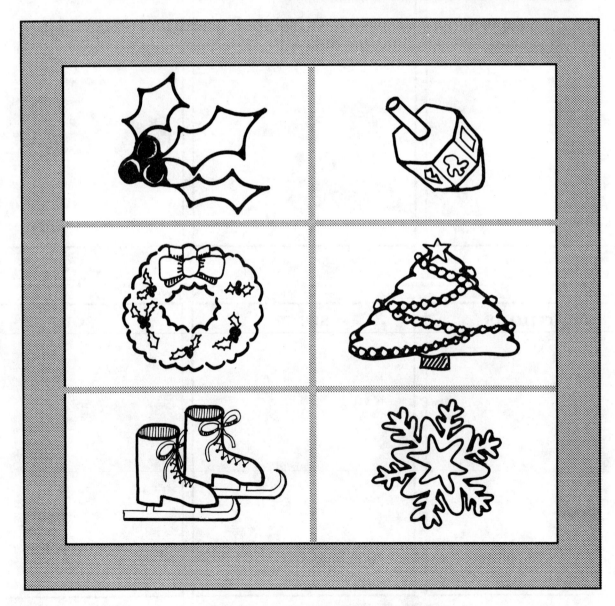

Hats Off to Holidays

Make a bulletin board of student-created hats that are associated with holidays, celebrations and multi-cultural events in the United States and around the world.

Leave room underneath each hat for student writing projects.

- a creative story
- a sentence describing the hat
- a paragraph about someone who might have worn the hat

Some suggestions to get you started:

- Pilgrim hat
- Bunny ears
- Elf/leprechaun hat
- Santa Hat
- Witch's hat
- Easter bonnet
- Tri-cornered patriot hat
- Indian headdress

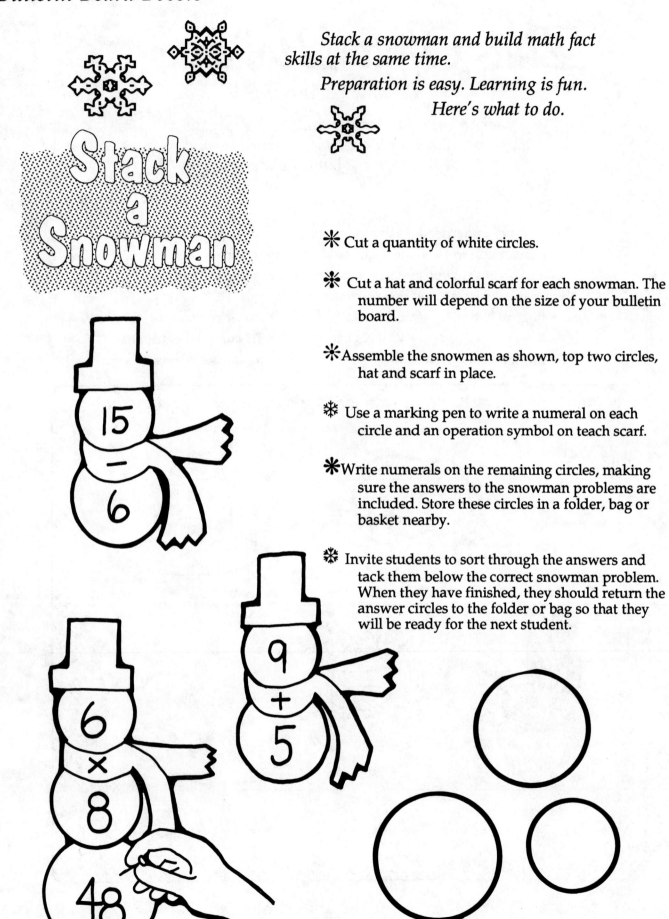

Stack a snowman and build math fact skills at the same time.

Preparation is easy. Learning is fun.

Here's what to do.

✳ Cut a quantity of white circles.

✳ Cut a hat and colorful scarf for each snowman. The number will depend on the size of your bulletin board.

✳ Assemble the snowmen as shown, top two circles, hat and scarf in place.

✳ Use a marking pen to write a numeral on each circle and an operation symbol on teach scarf.

✳ Write numerals on the remaining circles, making sure the answers to the snowman problems are included. Store these circles in a folder, bag or basket nearby.

✳ Invite students to sort through the answers and tack them below the correct snowman problem. When they have finished, they should return the answer circles to the folder or bag so that they will be ready for the next student.

PICK A
HOLIDAY
POCKET

Turn file folders into interactive holiday bulletin boards. Just follow the easy steps below.

Staple closed the two open sides of three file folders.

Cover the folder s with wrapping paper or construction paper decorated with symbols to suit the season or holiday.

Attach the folders, back side only, to a backed bulletin board.

Fill the pocket s with these suggestions:

Halloween—
— directions for drawing a monster
— names of costumes to be illustrated
— several books about ghosts

Christmas—
— several versions of *The Night Before Christmas* by Clement Moore
— round paper circles to turn into decorated ornaments
— blank forms for letters to Santa Claus

Valentine's Day
— the name of a classmate to create a special valentine for
— construction paper hearts to decorate
— zip top bags of red hot candies to estimate and count

Bulletin Board Boosts

Here's are two, easy to make, interactive holiday bulletin boards.
Patterns follow.

- **Stretch** several yarn vines across the bulletin board. Label each with a part of speech.
- **Cut** orange paper pumpkins. Write words on each.
- **Provide** clothespins. Students hang pumpkins on correct vine.

PART OF SPEECH PUMPKINS

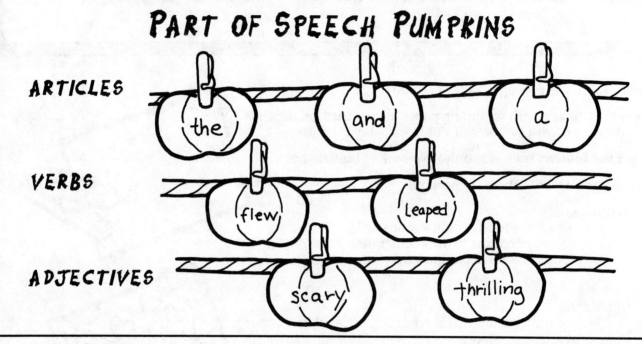

- **Build** a chimney using construction paper rectangles. Cut stockings from colorful paper, too.
- **Cut** out text from old books, magazines or newspapers. Glue each text block to a stocking.
- **Students read** text on stockings and use push pins to tack the stockings to the chimney in sequential order from left to right.

SEQUENCING STOCKINGS

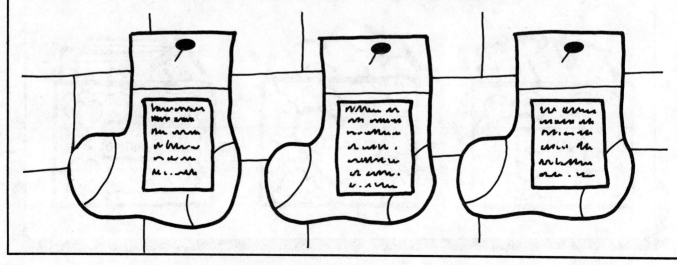

Use these patterns to make interactive
bulletin boards, previous page.

PUMPKIN

STOCKING

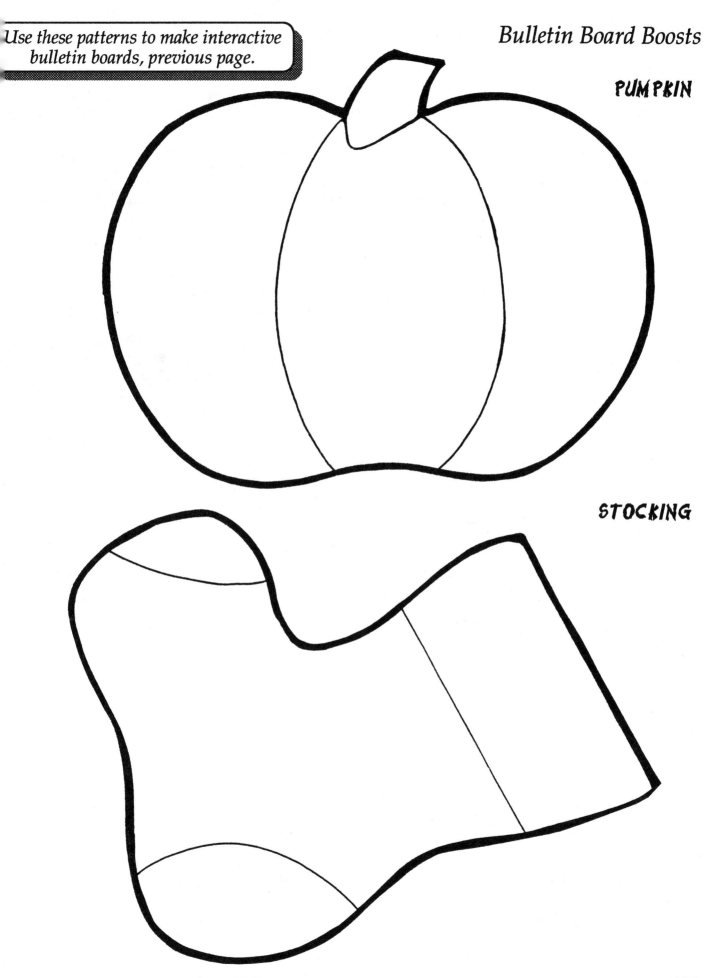

─ A Phrase for a Start ...─
...A Finish with Art

Start with a familar holiday or seasonal phrase cut from colorful construction paper. Ask children to visualize what they think of when they hear the phrase.

Stock a table with a variety of art supplies and let imaginations—and creativity— run free. Display all artwork around the phrase.

HO-HO-HO!

Here are some ideas to get you started:

Hippity-Hop

Lazy Days of Summer

Kiss the Blarney Stone

𝔅𝔲𝔫𝔫𝔶 𝔥𝔬𝔭

Trick or Treat

HAPPY HOLIDAYS

TURKEY TROT

You are my Sunshine

A Prop for a Start ...
...A Finish with Art

Start with a familar holiday or seasonal prop or shape cut from colorful construction paper or other material. Ask children to something specific ... but their own design.

Stock a table with a variety of art supplies and let imaginations—and creativity— run free. Display all artwork in or around the prop.

Here are some props to get you started:

Weave a Giant Easter Basket ...
    add some painted eggs or treats

SPIN A WEB OF CREPE PAPER ...
    ADD A GROUP OF SPIDERS

Design a huge trick or treat bag ...
    collect some goodies

Grow a graceful Christmas Tree ...
    paint some sparkling ornaments

Prepare paper soil for planting ...
    bloom a garden of flowers

Make an oversized envelope...
    design orignial stamps

Designer Showcase

Think solids, stripes, plaids , polka dots and frills. Just don't think ordinary.

Create designer versions of these holiday standbys.

Showcase your designer creations in a student-created designer border!

Here are some suggestions:

- turkey feathers
- nose for Rudolph
- pumpkin

- egg
- valentine heart
- Christmas tree topper

Turn spelling and sentence skill drill into an enjoyable event with this bulletin board.

"Turn over a ...

insect

"I saw an <u>insect</u> in the garden."

... and make a sentence."

- Just add a shape appropriate to the season or holiday.
  For example:
  leaf
  ladybug
  heart
  pumpkin
  sun

- Write a related holiday or seasonal word on the back of each. During class, ask a student to go to the bulletin board and "Turn over a ..."

- The child selects a shape, turns it over, reads the word—with or without help— and creates a sentence that contains the word.

- This bulletin board could stay up all year—just change the shapes and the words.

Vacation Picture Award

Paste a picture from your vacation, here.

Write a sentence about it below.

Thanks for sharing it with us.

_____

_____

_____

Name

Sweet Tooth Certificate

This certificate is awarded to you for trying to list at least 25 holiday treats and sweets.

Inventive Incentive

Reproduce and cut out the ghost below to hang over the desk of each student who contributes something special to the class during the month of October.

The contribution might be in the form of super work, citizenship, or improvement.

Clip a Coupon

Cupid's Coupon

Trade for one Valentine Treat

Name:

Turn In for an EGG-citing *Gift*

Name:

GOOD FOR ONE

STOCKING STUFFER

Name:

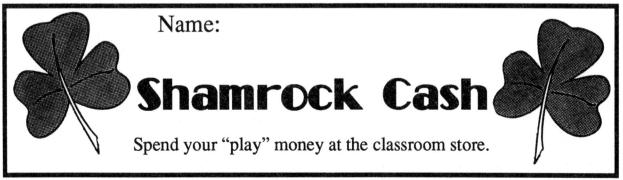

Name:

Shamrock Cash

Spend your "play" money at the classroom store.

NIFTY NOTES

from your teacher

Here are some notes to photocopy, cut apart and give to students. This page has pre-written messages. Blank notes on which to create your own message are on the following page. Take your pick—then pick up a student's spirits.

Santa Says ...

"You could lead my sleigh!"

You've stolen my heart!

Thanks. You're full of great ideas!

Thank You

I appreciate your hard work.

It's no Trick!

You're a Treat.

Trade this for a treat.

NIFTY NOTES
from your teacher

EGG-citing News Just for You!

_____

_____

_____

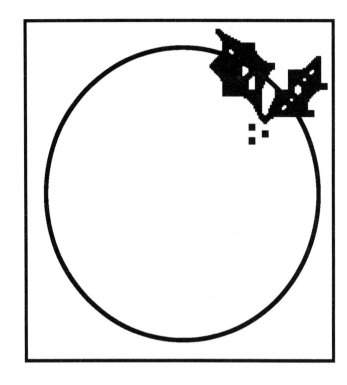

Read a Holiday Book

Get a Holiday Treat

Here's a reading incentive program that rewards students for each holiday book read. Read the suggestions below to find out how to to implement it.

Getting Ready

Reproduce a copy of the incentive form, following page, for each student.

Discuss the goal—Read a book, fiction or non-fiction, related to each holiday listed on the form.

Explain the form—Discuss the information required for each book. Practice writing a short summary together.

Share the reward—Tell them what they might expect for a completed book and summary.

Helpful Hints

Provide a list of suggested reading from which students may select the books to read.

Invite the school librarian to share recommended books with students.

Set up a display of books from which students may choose.

Discuss the difference between the fiction and non-fiction titles.

What to Reward

Offer a reward after each book is read and summarized. Make the reward relate, in some way, to the holiday. Choose stickers, food items or bookmarks. *For example:*

- For Christmas you might present a small ornament or candy cane.
- Valentine's Day books might be rewarded small chocolate hearts or heart stickers.
- Halloween literature readers might receive a special trick-or-treat bag or small bag of pumpkin seed snacks.

Read a Holiday Book   Get a Holiday Treat

Read a book, fiction or non-fiction, for each of the holidays below.
List the title and author. Write a short summary.

When you complete each book, show your teacher this form.
You will get a holiday treat or surprise for your effort.

Halloween

Book Title:

Author:
Short summary:

Thanksgiving
Book Title:

Author:
Short summary:

Christmas

Book Title:

Author:
Short summary:

Chanukah
Book Title:

Author:
Short summary:

Valentine's Day

Book Title:

Author:
Short summary:

Easter

Book Title:

Author:
Short summary:

INDEX

More Exciting Titles from Edupress

102 Indian Activity Book
Art•Crafts•Cooking

126 Colonial Activities
Art•Crafts•Cooking

138 Frontier Activities
Art•Crafts•Cooking

128 Easy Book Projects
Report, explore, share

134 Holiday Games
Fun-filled learning

135 Center Games
Ten easy game centers

136 Outdoor Games
Group and skill games

137 Desktop Games
Indoor learning games

140 Classroom Kickoff
Year-long resource

139 Super Arts & Crafts
Over 700 art activites

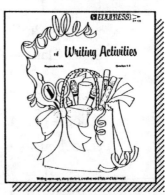

134 Oodles of Writing
Hundreds of prompts

127 Report Roundup
Research & report forms

130 Fall Projects
Multicurricular learning

131 Winter Projects
Loads of winter activities

132 Spring Projects
Apr/May/June fun

117 Wonders of Mystery
Theme units